The
Moral
Law

The
Moral
Law

Ernest Kevan

Sovereign Grace Publishers, Inc.
P.O. Box 4998
Lafayette, IN 47903

ISBN 1-58960-055-X

Printed In the United States of America
By Lightning Source, Inc.

Contents

CHAPTER I

INTRODUCTION

The purpose of this volume is to present a discussion of the value of the Law of God in the life of the believer, a subject of importance and urgency in these days. At various periods in the history of Christian doctrine it has become necessary to reaffirm the truth that the ministry of the Law has been Divinely ordained as a means of grace for the sanctification and godly walk of the believer. This, of course, carries with it no denial that the only sufficient power for sanctification is the indwelling life of Christ in the believer by the Holy Spirit: this is sanctification through faith, and it is one of the great glories of the Christian Gospel that it does not merely tell men to be good but enables them to be so.

But the bestowal of the power for a holy life needs to be accompanied by instruction in the pattern of it. In what does sanctified behaviour consist? It consists in pleasing God. What is it that pleases God? The doing of His will. Where is His will to be discerned? In His holy Law. The Law, then, is the Christian's rule of life, and the believer finds that he delights in the Law of God after the inward man (Romans vii. 22). The Christian is not lawless (ἄνομος) but "under the law to Christ," a phrase from Paul which would be more accurately rendered "in the law (ἔννομος) to Christ" (I Corinthians ix. 21). Sin is lawlessness (ἀνομία), and salvation is the bringing of the lawless one into his true relation to God, within the blessedness of His holy Law. The Law of Moses is none other than the Law of Christ.

The fact that by grace a man does not steal, or lie, or commit adultery, in no way destroys the fact that he must not, and the Christian who does any of these things becomes convicted by the Law as a sinner. Because he is a justified believer, this sin of his does not bring him into eternal condemnation, but it most certainly brings him under the disapprobation of the Lord. That God sees no sin in the believer is true in so far as his standing (justification) is concerned, but it is a quite incorrect proposition so far as his state (sanctification) is concerned. The Law of God, therefore, not only instructs the believer in that kind of life which is well-pleasing to God, but is the humbling instrument by which the Holy Spirit leads the believer to discover his shortcomings, to grieve over them, to repent of them, and so to apply himself to the Lord Jesus Christ in whom alone the grace of sanctification is found.

There would be fewer moral tragedies among professing Christians if the salutary instruction of the Law of God were more conscientiously heeded. Let the believer look alone to Christ for the enabling power of a victorious life -- as indeed he must -- but let him at the same time remember that holy living consists not in emotional delight but in keeping the commandments of God.

To insist upon this function of the Law of God in the life of the believer is not to become legalistic. Legalism is an abuse of the Law: it is a reliance on law-keeping for acceptance with God, and the proud or the servile observance of laws is no part of the grace of God. The joyfully rendered obedience of love, however, is a quite different thing and is of the very essence of Christian life. For a man to obey God because he loves to do so is not legalism; it is liberty: but, let it be remembered, it is still obedience.

The Law of God has its place in Christian experience because, although it is out of a deep love for God that the believer does the things which please Him, he is at the same time doing that which God commands him to do. If a man's unwillingness to obey does not nullify the commandment -- and this is conceded by all -- then neither does his willingness. Law does not end when a man delights to obey it: it is still there to be honoured and enjoyed in the obeying of it. A sovereign is no less a sovereign because his subjects love him. God does not cease to be God as soon as His people are reconciled to Him; He does not forfeit all rights to command as soon as people come to love Him. There is, therefore, nothing incompatible between love and obedience; for in the truly sanctified life there is loving obedience and obedient love.

This truth is grasped more easily, perhaps, if it is illustrated in respect of positive Law, as distinguished from moral Law. One of the outstanding instances of positive Law in the life of the child of God is, of course, the ordinance of the Lord's Supper. A believer will gladly keep this commandment of Christ, but he will never think of saying that he does so, not because the Lord commanded it, but merely because he likes to do it. If he were to speak like this he would then become a law to himself. The believer will say that he loves to keep every sacred command of Christ, and, in affirming this, he will recognise the place of the commandment. True godliness will not hold back to consider merely the intrinsic qualities of good or evil, but will give heed solely to the will of Him who has given the commandment. There is no holiness where there is not subjection to God: all goodness must be for God's sake, not for its own. The good works of the believer are not merely good, they are good in that they are owed. The obligation of obedience is

perpetual and belongs to man's creaturely relation
to God, and it is one of the richest fruits of grace
that a regenerate soul is able to say, "O how love I
thy law!" (Psalm cxix. 97) The Biblical doctrine of
sanctification, then, is not "rely and relax" but
"trust and obey". Puritan teaching avoids Pelagian
activism on the one hand and Quietest passivism on
the other, and in place of both of these it affirms
the necessity for the obedience of faith.

The further purpose of this volume is to present
the discussion of the Law through one of the finest
minds of the Puritan period, namely, that of Anthony
Burgess.

Much good Puritan thinking is to be found, not only
in the writings of the more well-known men, such as
John Owen and Thomas Goodwin, but also in the work
of those who are less familiar at the present time.
They have remained unknown largely on account of
a literary style of their period, which modern read-
ers find difficult to follow, but they were men of
theological perception, of brilliant intellect, clear
thinking and invincible argument. Anthony Burgess
was one of these.

The present treatment of the subject is based on
the insights and the material of this clear thinker
which are to be found in his remarkable work en-
titled, "**Vindiciae Legis**, or A Vindication of the
Morall Law". In this way it is hoped that to some
extent the great contribution made by Anthony Burgess may be salvaged and given its place in the
thought of today.

CHAPTER II

THE PERFECTION OF THE LAW

The study of the Law of God in the life of the believer has not been without its difficulties, but to some extent this has been due to an absence of attention to certain basic considerations. There are, therefore, several important guiding principles to be borne in mind in the exposition of the doctrine of the Law.

The first of these has to do with the meaning of the word "law". Confusion arises if the word is thought of only in its English use, or if its meaning is restricted to the Greek and Latin words νόμος and lex, which signify an authoritative rule of duty. The Old Testament word torah includes much more than these ideas, and signifies not only what is to be done, but also what is to be known. It stands for Divinely revealed instruction, whether it be in the form of doctrine, exhortation, promise or command. This is why the Mosaic Law can be called a covenant, and, conversely, why the Mosaic Covenant can be spoken of as the Law. It is in this comprehensive sense also that Paul is able to use the term in such a figurative expression as "the law of faith" (Romans iii. 27).

There are other meanings of the word "law" which belong not to its derivation, but to its use. Sometimes it signifies any part of the Old Testament, as in the saying of Christ, which, with a particular reference to a psalm (Psalm lxxxii. 6) nevertheless reads, "Is it not written in your law, I said, Ye are gods?" (John x. 34) Sometimes the phrase "the law and the prophets" (Matthew vii. 12; Luke xvi. 16) is used to indicate all the books of the

Old Testament. Occasionally the word "law" is used for only the ceremonial aspects of worship, as in the expression, "The law having a shadow of good things to come" (Hebrews x. 1). In some places it is used for that revelation of Himself which God gave peculiarly to the Israelites, as for example, in the words, "for the law was given by Moses, but grace and truth came by Jesus Christ" (John i. 17); and in yet further passages it is used as a description of the Jews in their condition without Christ, a use which Paul makes in the epistles to the Romans (iii. 19) and to the Galatians (iii. 10; iv. 21).

Before any valid discussion of the doctrine of the Law can take place, and certainly before any arguments can be brought against the Law, it must first be shown in what sense the word is being used; for Paul argues against the Law in one sense, and pleads for it in another.

A second guiding principle is the necessity to recognise that there is nothing contradictory in the doing of a thing out of love and also in obedience to the Law. It is occasionally contended that obedience to law is slavish, whereas the believer is moved by love and needs no law. This, of course, contains within it a logical contradiction, besides being completely untrue in experience. It is fallacious to put the cause and the result into opposition. To suggest that there is a contradiction between the motive by which the believer pleases God and the things which are themselves pleasing to Him is illogical, for the Spirit of God moves the heart to love and delight in that which He commands. Adam is an instance of this, for while he was yet unfallen he obeyed out of love, but also because of the command. The angels obey the commandments of God (otherwise the apostate angels could not have sinned), and yet they do all things in love.* The supreme instance

* The mother of Moses provides a tender human illustration,

of all is Christ Himself upon whom a commandment was laid, yet He fulfilled it out of love.** The inference to be drawn from this, therefore, is that to do a thing out of obedience to a command, simply because it is a command, does not necessarily imply the absence of love. The obedience of a servant need not be servile obedience.

In the third place, it must be carefully observed that Christ's full obedience to the Law for the justification of sinners does not exempt the believer from obedience to it for ends other than justification. It is one of the basic truths of the Gospel that no man can offer his good deeds as the ground of his justification, but it is a great mistake to infer from this that because the works of the Law do not justify they are needless. This would be good reasoning if a believer obeyed the Law for the same end that Christ did, but that is impossible. An analogy may be drawn from the Christian experience of suffering. Christ suffered as He bore the curse of the Law, and thereby freed the believer from all punishment; yet the believer may endure suffering for other ends. In the same way it may be argued that the believer performs the works of God's Law for other ends than Christ did them, and the obligation

for she nursed her son out of motherly love for him, but it was also in obedience to the commandment of Pharaoh's daughter.

** Sometimes this last instance is challenged, and the question is raised whether Christ had a command laid upon Him by the Father; but the complete answer to this is given in the Scripture which provides evidence of it in many places. Indeed, if a commandment were not laid upon Christ it would not be possible to speak of an obedience of Christ, for obedience relates to a command.

resting on the believer to perform acts of obedience must not be misconstrued in support of a doctrine of justification by works.

A fourth guiding principle in framing a doctrine of the Law of God in the life of the believer is that of the necessity to draw a distinction between a believer and his personal acts. Although it is true that the Law does not condemn the believer, in view of his being in a state of grace, yet the sins he commits are condemned and they are deserving of God's wrath. It is therefore a foolish comparison to say with one of the older antinomian writers that a man under grace has no more to do with the law "than an Englishman has with the laws of Spain". For although every believer is in a state of grace, so that his person is justified, yet, so far as he commits sins, those are as much condemned in him as they are in another. There may be the acceptance of the person by the grace of God, though there be at the same time the disapproval of the things he does.

A final principle to be borne in mind is that the Law is not to be rejected because man has no power to keep it. When the rejection of the Law is argued on this ground, it is often forgotten that, similarly, man has no power to obey the Gospel. The command to believe is as impossible as the command to obey, and so the Gospel seems to speak just such impossible things as does the Law. Absence of ability does not infer absence of obligation.

With these important considerations made clear, it is possible to exhibit the goodness of the Law. If God is good, His Law must be good. This is the experience of the psalmist when he exclaims, "O how love I thy law" (Psalm cxix. 97), and this, likewise, is the conviction of Paul when he says to Timothy, "We know that the law is good" (I Timothy i. 8).

The goodness of the Law of God makes itself known in many ways, as a brief survey of it will show.

First of all, the Law of God is good in its contents, that is to say, in its spiritual significance. There can be no question that it is good to love God and to trust in Him; and these are precisely the things that are commanded in the Law. All goodness is summed up in the Law, and there is nothing that can be conceived of as good which is not contained within it.

Second, the Law of God is good in its Divine authority. It is this Divine authority which makes it binding on men. God's authority is in the Law in two ways: first, in the rightness of what He wills, and second, in His act of willing the things that are right. If the things commanded in the Law are examined, it will be seen that the justice of some of them arises out of the simple fact that God wills them; that is to say, in themselves the things may not bear any evidence of being either intrinsically good or intrinsically bad, but they are constituted so by God. Things commanded in this way are usually described as belonging to what is known as positive Law. There are other things commanded by God which are in themselves just, and God wills them for that reason. The justness of these things, of course, must not be thought of as it if were a quality standing over God and outside of Him; it is itself nothing other than the manifested perfection of God Himself. These just things that God wills derive their quality of being just from their agreement with that eternal justice and goodness which are in God. On account of this it is impossible that such a Divinely authoritative Law should be abrogated, for this would be to deny the justice and goodness of God. The obligation that comes by the Law is eternal and unchangeable, insomuch that it implies an

absolute contradiction to say that there can be a
righteousness in man apart from subjection to the
command of God. The essence of the goodness of
the Law is its relation to the authority of God.

In the next place, it has to be said that the Law
is good in its use. It has a double use, as the Holy
Spirit employs it as an instrument for the conversion of sinners and as a means to stir up the heart
of a believer to his duty (Psalm xix. 7-11; cxix. 93).
Sometimes objection is taken to this truth about
the use of the Law on the ground that the word "law"
does not in every instance of its use mean the Ten
Commandments, but quite often stands more broadly
for the teaching which the Word of God contains.
That is true, of course, but the admission of this
does not involve the exclusion of the injunctions of
the moral Law, for they were the most important
of them all. Most of the objections that are raised
against the usefulness of the Law are based on the
mistake of thinking of the Law as operating alone,
and then drawing a contrast between the alleged
power of the Gospel and the weakness of the Law.
But it is an unreasonable thing to conceive of the
Law apart from the Spirit of God, and then to com-
pare it with the Gospel; for if the Gospel itself --
even its promises of mercy and forgiveness -- were
to be thought of apart from the Spirit, it would
achieve nothing: indeed, by itself it would be as
much a dead letter as the Law. But neither Law nor
Gospel is a dead letter, for the Holy Spirit makes
use of both in a saving manner.

Further, the Law is good in the sanctions by which
it is strengthened. It is supported by the promises
of God, which promises are not only temporal, as
in the Fifth Commandment, but also spiritual, as in
the Second Commandment. None will question, of
course, that the righteousness of the Law and that
of the Gospel differ widely, and that their delimita-
tion is one of the hardest tasks of theology, but this

does not justify the denial of truly spiritual blessings under the Law. It is a mistake to say that
the Law has only material blessings and promises
of this present world*; for it is evident from the
Old Testament that the believers of those days had
for substance the same faith as the Christian believer today. If, however, Law and Gospel be taken
in such an artificial way as to say that all commandments, wherever they are found, must belong
to the Law, and all promises, whether found in the
Old or New Testament, must be attributed to the
Gospel, then the Law can have no sanction by promise. But no such arbitrary definition can be shown
in Scripture, for the Law is always an instrument
of grace and its demands have the sanction of mer-
ciful promises.**

Again, the Law is good in its functions. These
functions include the declaration of what is the will
of God; the command of obedience to this will; the
invitation by promise; the compulsion by warning;
and the condemnation of those who transgress. The
Law exercises these functions against the ungodly,
and some of these cannot be denied even with respect to the godly. In the interests of a denial of
the claims of the Law on the life of the believer, it
is sometimes alleged that the Law must always condemn and that this is a sine qua non of the Law. But
this is an astonishing assertion, for how can it be

---

* This was the error of the Manichaeans and the Marcion-
ites.

** When the sanction of the Law by promise is spoken of, the
Law is being referred to in its evangelical Mosaic administration and not as it was given to Adam, with a promise of eternal
life upon perfect obedience. Such apostolic expressions as, "To
him that worketh the reward is reckoned of debt", and "the doers
of the law are justified", must be understood to be said of the
Law as given to Adam, not of the Mosaic covenant.

thought to apply to the Law given to Adam in the period of his innocence? The angels also must have been under a Law, else they could not have sinned; yet it was not a condemning Law before they fell. If condemning be taken potentially, then, it is true, the Law is always condemning; but it is not always actually so. The functions of the Law are good in themselves and are not by any means to be confined to that of condemning the wrong-doer.

Finally, the Law is good in its end. It is intended to lead to Christ (Romans x. 4), and it finds its fulfilment in Him.

This survey of the goodness of the Law leads by a natural transition of thought to an inquiry into the purposes of the Law. These purposes relate both to the ungodly and to the believer.

So far as the ungodly are concerned the Law has two purposes: first, to restrain sin, and second, to condemn the sinner. As to the former of these, it is not possible to go so far as saying that the Law is capable of changing men's hearts, but it nevertheless performs a valuable service as an external instrument by means of which they are kept in a kind of outward conformity to what is right. By its positive instruction and its solemn warning, it keeps men back from much flagrant evil, and it was this use of the Law which made the apostle say that the Law "was added because of transgressions" (Galatians iii. 19). The second purpose of the Law toward the ungodly is to condemn them for their transgression of it. The curse of the Law is the sore displeasure of God, and this accompanies every breach of it.

The purpose of the Law to the believer is fourfold. It stimulates resistance to sin, it reveals inward corruption, it destroys self-righteousness, and it increases esteem of Christ.

Although it is true that "the law is not made for a righteous man" (I Timothy i. 9), yet, because no

believer is perfectly righteous, and because there
is no one who does not need to confess the weakness
of his love for God and the feebleness of his delight
in holy things, it becomes a fact of spiritual experience that the Law of God, by commanding, stirs the
believer to a resistance of evil and a zealous seeking
after godliness. Not only the untamed colt, but also
the trained horse, needs a bit and bridle; and so not
only the ungodly, but even the godly, whose hearts
have been much broken and tamed, still need a
bridle, lest they should cast off the Spirit of God.
Any who regard themselves as so established in
spiritual things as to say that they do not need this
are greatly in the dark about themselves. They
speak like this, not because they do not need it --
for they need it most -- but because they are not
aware of that need.'

Paul writes to the Romans (vii. 7-25) about the
continuing corruption in the heart of the believer,
and he explains that in his own case he discovered
this when the light of the Law shone into the secret
places of his heart. So blind is the sinful heart of
even the believer that he can never come to know
the depth of original sin and all the sinful desires
flowing from it except by means of the Law. It was
for this reason that Paul writes, "I had not known
sin, but by the law" (Romans vii. 7), meaning by this
that the Law of Nature was so obliterated that it
could not show a man even the least part of the corruption of his heart. The Law is the mirror in which
the believer is permitted to see himself.

The effects of this revelation to the believer of
the sinfulness of his own heart are seen in a deep
sense of shame and humility. When the believer per-
ceives that his very best attainment comes short of
the requirements of the Law, that the earth is not
more distant from heaven than he is from righteousness, this drives him to abandon all confidence in

his performance of religious good works. Paul exemplifies this when he says he consents to the Law and delights in it, but cannot reach to the righteousness of it, and so exclaims, "O wretched man that I am!" (Romans vii. 24) How apt are even the best of men to be proud and secure, as David and Peter were, but a recollection of the holy demands of the Law will keep the believer humble. It is quite beside the mark, then, to say that the preaching of the Law leads men to trust in themselves and to adhere to their own righteousness; for there is no more certain way to bring men to see their spiritual poverty and their guilt, than by showing them the strict and exacting demands of the Law.

In the wonderful wisdom of God the Law is an instrument of grace, and the Holy Spirit by the Law reduces the believer to this deep shame and humility only to lead him to value the person and work of the Lord Jesus Christ the more highly. It is to this place that Paul is brought in the great agony of striving with the inward corruption of his heart, and he triumphantly cries, "I thank God through Jesus Christ" (Romans vii. 25). It is true that sometimes an overwhelming sense of sin seems to destroy all hope in the convicted believer's heart, but this is only a temporary effect of the Law and is not its ultimate intention. The Law constantly strips the believer of his self-righteousness and so increases his esteem for the righteousness which is to be found in Christ (Philippians iii. 9).

A true understanding of what the Law of God is, together with an appreciation of its intrinsic goodness and its Divine purpose, will compel the recognition of the value of the Law.

The spiritual value of the Law of God cannot be denied. Shall it be said that because the Law is not good for justification it is in no sense good for anything else? Is gold valueless because a man cannot eat it? The Gospel requirement of faith may serve as an illustration of this. If faith be regarded as a "work", it does not justify; but because faith looked upon in this way does not justify, is the act of believing to be rejected? Certainly not! In like manner there is to be no rejection of the continuing value of the Law of God, even though no sinner may hope for justification by appealing to it.

The Law has value as a means of grace, and to destroy the Law is to destroy the grace of Christ. It is utterly mistaken to suppose that there is any kind of opposition between them.* Who prizes the city of refuge so much as the wrong-doer who is pursued by guilt? Who desires the brasen serpent as he who has been stung by the fiery serpent? If Christ is the end of the Law, in the sense of its fulfilment, how can He be regarded as contrary to it? Further, if the Law of God and the grace of God could co-exist under the Old Covenant, why not under the New? Opposition between Law and grace arises only when there is abuse of either or both of them. There is no doubt that if a man uses the Law otherwise than God has appointed, he must not be surprised if it becomes hurtful to him; but if he so uses the Law that Christ becomes more and more his trust, and grace becomes the more welcome to him, then he does well.

Without fear of contradiction, therefore, it may be affirmed that the sublime perfection of the Law presents the believer with a challenge to his thought, a claim upon his affections, and a demand upon his obedience.

---

* Justification by Law and justification by grace are most certainly opposed, but that is a quite different subject from an opposition between Law and Grace.

CHAPTER III

HOW THE LAW IS TO BE USED

It is possible to use the law wrongly, and Paul draws attention to this when he completes his sentence about the goodness of the Law by adding, "if a man use it lawfully" (I Timothy i. 8). The goodness of the Law is experienced only as the Law is put to its proper use and when it is seen in relation to the end for which it is given; for the Law becomes anything but good to those who misuse it. It becomes a burden too heavy to bear, and ultimately a curse, for example, to the man who seeks justification by his endeavours at Law-keeping. Because of wrong conceptions of the purpose of the Law, it is sometimes thought that the Law is an evil from which men need to be set free, whereas it is not the Law but "the curse of the Law" from which Christ redeems the believer. Christ delivers the sinner, not from the spiritual obligations of God's holy Law, but from the evil that he has brought upon himself by his misuse of the Law.

Man's fundamental abuse of the Law is to put it into opposition to Christ for justification, and to regard Law-keeping as an alternative ground of acceptance before God. This was the basic error of those Jews of New Testament times who went about "to establish their own righteousness" (Romans x. 1f.). The temptation that came to the Galatians was to make a kind of compromise by relying, not only on the saving work of Christ, but also on their own good religious deeds. But to place an alternative by the side of that which is declared to be the only way of salvation is to put it in opposition. There can no more be two things to justify than there can be two suns in the heavens. The Law and Christ are not partners in the sinner's justification, nor are they to be equally joined together, for the Law is subordinate to Christ. If it be remembered that the Law is related to the Gospel as means are to the end, then not only will the true function of the Law be seen, but the mistake will be avoided of elevating the Law above its proper use.

The natural man finds nothing easier than this abuse of the law; indeed, it is one of the evidences of the corruption of man's heart that he has the inveterate habit of turning every good gift of God to wrong purposes. It therefore requires the renewing of a man's mind to enable him to perceive that the Law cannot possibly provide the sinner with a way of acceptance with God.

Serious consequences follow from the abuse of the Law in this manner, not the least of which is that it destroys the nature of grace. Justification by grace is completely exclusive of the merit of good works: it excludes not only the works of the law which a man might try to perform in his own sinful condition, but also those which are performed by the believer through the indwelling grace of God. There is total incompatibility between the principle of works and the principle of grace, and Paul does not allow any modification of this even in the interests of the alleged meritorious works of grace. Further, that legalistic works are opposed to grace is clear from the use of the word grace in Scripture for the unmerited favour of God. The failure to distinguish between the grace of God that accepts the sinner and the effects of that grace in the sinner's life, leads to the mistake of stressing inward holiness as if it possessed some saving virtue. At the same time, in the realm of spiritual experience, confusion of this kind occasions much distress to

the contrite believer who knows himself to be not
so holy as he desires to be.

A second consequence of this wrong use of the
Law is that it denies the sufficiency of the work of
Christ. It was in this way that those who troubled
the Galatians made Christ void and fell away from
Him (Galatians v. 4). An endeavour has sometimes
been made to blunt the edge of Paul's argument
against the works of the Law by affirming that he
is speaking only of the ceremonial Law; but this
reasoning cannot bear inspection. It is true that
the earlier discussions of the Jerusalem Council
(Acts xv. 1-41) were about the necessity of Jewish
ceremonies such as circumcision; but in the letters
to the Galatians (iii. 6-9) and Romans (iv. 1-8) Paul
goes behind these ceremonial rites to all works
whatsoever, and proceeds to exclude from justification even Abraham's works and David's. Christ
would be no Christ if works were the basis of righteousness; because the righteousness "which is
through the faith of Christ" is set by Paul over
against his "own righteousness" (Philippians iii. 9)
and is called "the righteousness of God" (Romans
x. 3). If good works justify a man, what need is
there for a Saviour? The sufficiency of Christ for
salvation is directly repudiated by any reliance on
the Law for justification.

It follows from the foregoing that any appeal to
the merit of Law-keeping destroys the true doctrine
of justification. This is not the place to expound
that doctrine in any detail, but it must be remembered that the Scripture speaks of justification not
as an infusion into man of that which is perfect,
but an acceptance of the man -- even though sinful
in himself -- on account of the righteousness of
Christ. The language of David expresses this perfectly and is taken up by Paul: "Blessed is the man
unto whom the Lord imputeth not iniquity" (Psalm

xxxii. 2; Romans iv. 7, 8). There is some difference
of opinion among theologians about the imputation of
Christ's active righteousness to the believer, and
that need not detain the discussion now; but there
is no doubting that, in the Scripture, justification,
negatively expressed, is that act of God by which He
does not reckon a man's sins against him. It is also
perfectly clear from Scripture that justification is
not the acceptance of holiness from the sinner, but
the declaration by God to the sinner that his sins
are put away. Man is certainly not justified by an
inherent righteousness of his own, for this would
lead either to an extreme perfectionism, or to that
state of things in which a man may never know that
he is justified until he is dead. Justification becomes
confused with sanctification when it is said to be
based on inherent righteousness; and, further, it is
quite incorrect to say that because sin is covered
by God's justifying act, there is therefore no sin to
be found in the believer. Arguments of this kind are
completely demolished by Paul (Romans vii. 7-25).
The covering of sin in justification refers to its
guilt, but sanctification has to do with the breaking
of its reigning power. Besides, justification by
works, or by inherent righteousness of any kind,
must regard the justified man as godly at the mo-
ment of the Divine act of grace, whereas the Scripture speaks of him as ungodly (Romans iv. 5).

It is evident also that reliance on the works of
the Law destroys the place of faith in justification.
When the all-sufficiency of Christ is set aside, and
when grace is nullified, then justifying faith must
also be made void. There are three main causes
of justification which operate together: the grace of
God as the efficient, the blood and righteousness of
Christ as the meritorious, and faith as the instrumental; and although it would be wrong to put the
faith of the sinner on the same level as the merit of

the Saviour, yet both are equally necessary to bring
about the sinner's justification. It can be taken for
granted that faith is but the instrumental cause of
justification; for it would be a lapse into a doctrine
of justification by works to regard faith as the effectual cause, and far more so to think of it as the
meritorious cause. The value of faith as an instrument of justification is established by the fact that
an instrumental preposition is used with it in such
phrases as "through faith in his blood" (Romans
iii. 25) and "justified by faith" (Romans v. 1), and
it requires to be observed in passing that it is
never said, διά πιστίν, for faith, as if there were
dignity or merit in it; but always διά πίστεως,
through faith.

The use of the Law for justification has also evil
consequences of a practical kind, for the belief in
justification by works creates a sinful self-com-
placence in men. A man may exclude Christ from
his soul, not only by those that are commonly recognised as sins, but by self-confidence. "Ye are
they which justify yourselves" was the charge which
Christ brought against the Pharisees (Luke xvi. 15).
It is impossible not to see how afraid Paul was to
be found in his own righteousness, and it was this
which made Luther say, "Take heed, not only of thy
sins, but also of thy good duties". Paul makes it
clear that peace with God comes only through justification by faith, and no amount of patience, or repentance, or sufferings, or good works can procure
it. That which condemns a man cannot save him,
nor can that which disturbs him bring comfort to
him. To destroy faith is to destroy hope, and hope
is the strong support of a Christian. If hope be
placed in Christ and the promises, it is as firm as
faith, and for that reason Paul writes, "hope maketh
not ashamed" (Romans v. 5); but if a man's hope
were in himself, how often would he be cast down!

Finally, and most seriously of all, this self-confident abuse of the Law takes away the glory due to God. It was Abraham's faith that gave God glory. The unrenewed man cannot see any relation between believing in God and glorifying God; but the truth is that all a man's religious activity put together cannot give more glory to God than when he truly puts his trust in Him.

There is perfect harmony between the saving grace of God and the good works of the believer, but the exposition of that harmony constitutes one of the problems of Christian theology. It is by no means easy to insist upon the grace of God without giving some kind of foundation to the charge that the doctrine is licentious or antinomian; nor is it easy to affirm the necessity of good works without provoking the cry that the grace of God is being destroyed.

The former of these difficulties can be illustrated historically by a study of the Canons of Trent, which reveal a complete misunderstanding of the doctrine of justification by faith, and which charge the doctrines of grace with being antinomian. The following are some of the anathemas.

> Canon 19. If any man shall say that the ten commandments do not in anywise belong to Christians, let him be accursed.
> Canon 20. If any man shall hold that a justified person is not bound to the observance of the Commandments, but only to believe, let him be accursed.
> Canon 21. If any shall hold that Christ Jesus is given to men as a Redeemer in whom they are to trust, but not as a Law-giver whom they are to obey, let him be accursed.

The second problem can also be historically

illustrated, and, in this instance, it is found in the views of a group of early Antinomians in Europe, called Flacians, who went too far in their repudiation of good works. Thus, instead of maintaining the Scriptural position that good works were necessary to salvation, * they held that good works were pernicious to salvation. The misunderstanding centered in the necessity that was here asserted, and it was to this that the Flacians took strong exception. Melancthon and others found no difficulty in this statement, however, and understood the necessity to be a necessity, not of merit, but of presence. They held that no one was in a state of salvation in whose life there was not the evidence of good works.

It would be safe to say that if all the controversy that ensued had been inspired only by the desire to deter men from putting confidence in their good works, there would have been little cause for anxiety, but, unfortunately, the antinomian assertions were far more than an over-zealous pleading for the doctrine of grace. There was much more in the controversy than ill-advised language, and the conclusions which Antinomians drew from their peculiar interpretation of the doctrine of justification by faith were injurious in the extreme.**

A number of vital principles of the Gospel were at stake in this controversy, one of the most important of which had to do with the place of obedience and good works in the life of the believer. The

---

* In a sense properly to be defined.

** Antinomianism has never organised itself into an ecclesiastical form, as some of the other major theological alignments have done, but it is still extremely vocal in circles where a kind of non-theological biblicism prevails. The issues can best be discussed, however, by reference to the antinomian school of thought as it appeared in the Puritan period.

Antinomians denied that good works had any such place, and made full use of such Pauline statements as "a man is justified by faith without the deeds of the law" (Romans iii. 28). They held that by this statement Paul not only excludes works from having any power to justify the sinner, but that he repudiates them altogether. This denial by the Antinomians was, in turn, occasionally misrepresented by the orthodox Puritans who charged them with meaning that there was a general pardon for men even while they were purposing to continue in their sins. But this charge was a little unfair; for a careful examination of the writings of the antinomian authors reveals that their main concern was to extol the grace of God and to allow no place for the supposed merit of good works. In their right exaltation of free grace they were suspicious of any insistence on repentance and faith as pre-requisites for justification, and these were the good works which they excluded from God's act of justifying the sinner.

A second antinomian denial was that any gain or any loss could come to a believer by means of good works. The antinomian doctrine declared that "though there be sins committed, yet there is no peace broken, because the breach of peace is satisfied in Christ; there is a reparation of the damage before the damage itself be committed"; and again, "If a man expects to gain anything by his graces he will have nothing but knocks". It is agreed by all, and needs no discussion, that if a man expected to merit heaven or to secure pardon by any repentance or virtue of his own, this would show him to be grossly unaware of the imperfection of all human virtues and ignorant of the greatness of the Divine mercy.

The root of the problem resides in the possibility of thinking about the significance of good works in

a twofold way, and the opponents in this controversy would appear to have used the same terms
in two senses. The Antinomian was right when he
strenuously denied that there was any value in good
works as a contributory cause of a sinner's acceptance with God, and the orthodox Puritan agreed
with him unreservedly in this. At the same time,
the orthodox affirmed that no justified person could
be indifferent to good works, and that, though these
good works could have no place as the cause of the
sinner's justification, they were expected as the
result of it. They held that good works, though af-
fording no merit, nevertheless provided sound evidence of the sinner's standing before God. The value
of this evidence, and who they are to whom the evidence is submitted, constitute further questions,
but the insistence of the orthodox on the necessity
for good works in the justified believer was important in its own right. Their protest was against
what today would be called an easy "believism".
The arguments which they adduced were found first
of all in the severe and sharp threatenings which
Scripture expresses even to the godly when they
neglect to repent or when they go on in sin, for
example, "If ye live after the flesh, ye shall die"
(Romans viii. 13). If the Scripture threatens in this
way to men living in sin, it must surely also be
true that if they do not sin they may find comfort;
in other words, they may perceive some evidence
of the work of grace in their hearts. This is what
was meant by saying that the holy deeds of the believer had in them a promise of pardon and eternal
life; this was not because of their worth, but because of that to which their presence bore witness.
For this reason, they held, the godly might rejoice
when they found them in themselves.

The Antinomians countered this by a third denial,
namely, that good works were signs and testimonies

of grace. Their argument was that the only evidence the believer could have was twofold: the revealing of the Holy Spirit and the receiving of Christ by faith. Any other evidence of assurance that was sought, they said, was vitiated by the possibility of self-deception and the incompleteness of the work of sanctification in the believer. But the two evidences put forward by the Antinomians were not without their own dangers of subjectivity, and sometimes the former of these was so represented that it amounted to "revelations" which were quite independent of the written word. As to the evidence deriving from the receiving of Christ by faith, a man could as easily deceive himself about this as about the sincerity of his good works.

The grounds for denying the evidential value of good works were sought in a number of passages of Scripture, such as in the epistle to the Romans, for example, where it is said that God justifies the ungodly (Romans iv. 5). The reply to the antinomian inference drawn from this sentence was that the man who is justified is being considered in the state in which God finds him, not in the state to which He brings him. The man who is in himself ungodly is justified on the ground of Christ's merit and then is also made godly; though that godliness does not justify him. The adjective "ungodly" relates to the believer as he is in his own corrupt nature, but it indicates nothing concerning the work of God's grace: it merely underlines the truth that the subject of sanctification is a sinner. Much the same reply was made to the argument based on the words, "when we were enemies, we were reconciled to God by the death of his Son" (Romans v. 10), for it is clear that when a sinner believes he no longer remains at enmity with God. Again, it is said elsewhere that the Saviour receives gifts "for the rebellious also" (Psalm lxviii. 18); but here, too, it is obvious that the purport of the words is to show that even the most rebellious of men can be converted.

Let the law of God be used "lawfully", and not only will God be glorified in all His ways but the child of God also will find comfort and strength.

CHAPTER IV

THE GOOD WORKS OF THE BELIEVER

Upon what grounds are the people of God to be zealous of good works? Although the natural man finds it very hard to do good works without thinking of himself as doing these things for the purpose of justification, it is nevertheless true that the performance by grace of the good works of the Law is perfectly compatible with the Gospel doctrine of justification by faith.

The expression "good works" does not refer to the merely external actions of religion: it stands for the gifts of God's Spirit in the believer and the actions that flow from them. It is clear, therefore, that quite apart from any considerations of perfection, there is much need of the Holy Spirit's activity for even the beginnings of godly action. Some of the essentials of a truly godly action are that it must be commanded by God; it must be effected in the believer by the Spirit of God; it must flow from an inward principle of grace whereby a man is a new creature; and the end must be God's glory. The very best that the most purified man can do is but a glow-worm in its brightness, not a star; so that the action is good only when, being answerable to the rule, it is from God and through God and to God.

Unhappily, it is not possible to proceed far in the study of good works without encountering another of the antinomian paradoxes. Sometimes they spoke in a derogatory manner about good works, and regarded the endeavour to find spiritual evidences in the life as an unprofitable thing to do. On other occasions the Antinomians extolled good works so

highly that, by reason of Christ's imputed righteousness, they regarded all the believer's works perfect, and so applied the Scripture which speaks of
the Church as "without spot or wrinkle" (Ephesians
v. 27) to the present life. They spoke not only of a
righteousness or justification by imputation, but
also of saintship and holiness by this obedience of
Christ: and hence it was, they said, that God saw
no sin in unbelievers. Both of these paradoxical
extremes must be rejected as untrue.

When good works are said to be necessary, it is
important to define the end for which the necessity
is affirmed. Careful distinction must be made, for
example, between the statement that good works are
necessary to believers, and the statement that good
works are necessary to justification and salvation.
Although this second proposition is true in some
sense, yet, because the words are apt to give the
impression that holiness has some direct influence
upon a man's justification and salvation, it is
probably wiser not to use it.

Good works are necessary to the believer for
four reasons. First of all, they are necessary as
the believer's duty to God. The obligation of obedience is perpetual, not only by reason of the eternal
Law of God, but on account of the believer's indebt-
edness to His grace. The Law of God still remains
as a rule and directory for the believer's life and
the godly man delights in it (Romans vii. 22). If
Christ affirms that whoever breaks the least commandment shall be least in the kingdom of heaven
(Matthew v. 19), the teaching that advocates the
abolition of all of them must be regarded as quite
inexcusable. This necessity of duty relates to God's
glory, a glory which is manifested in the obedience
of His creatures. God is both pleased with the believer's godly actions -- even though they be imperfect -- and glorified by them.

Secondly, good works are necessary as the believer's evidence to himself about the reality of his salvation. "Give diligence to make your calling and election sure," says Peter (II Peter i. 10). The good works thus encouraged are not in themselves evidences of grace, but they become so by the Spirit of God who uses them as He "beareth witness with our spirit that we are the children of God" (Romans viii. 16). Good works are a condition without which a man cannot be saved. By this is meant that although a man cannot by the presence of such good works infer a cause of his salvation, yet by the absence of them he may conclude his condemnation. It is therefore quite false to say that good works do not profit the believer, nor bad hinder him; for the Scripture speaks so plainly to the contrary. "If ye live after the flesh, ye shall die", said Paul (Romans viii. 13), and the writer to the Hebrews urged them to "follow...holiness, without which no man shall see the Lord" (Hebrews xii. 14).

Good works are thus a kind of defence to the believer, and some of them are represented as a breastplate and a shield (Ephesians vi. 14,16). While it is true that Paul speaks of the might of the Lord in this connection and insists that prayer must be joined to these things, that does not deny the value of what is instrumental in the defence of the believer. It is for this reason that in the epistle to the Romans good works are called the armour or weapons of light (Romans xiii. 1-14). Luther observes, "He does not call the works of darkness, 'weapons' of darkness; but good works he calls weapons because we ought to use them as weapons to resist Satan". There is also, of course, a kind of fitness of things existing between good works on the one side and faith and the Holy Spirit on the other, and it is from this deep connection that Paul is able to speak of "faith which worketh by love" (Galatians v. 6).

It is sometimes thought to be a contradiction to say both that a sinner is justified by "faith only" and that unless his faith is working it cannot justify him, but there is no contradiction when these sayings are correctly understood. Paul and James are not at variance; for James brings the very same passage to prove Abraham was not justified by faith alone (James ii. 21-24) which Paul brings to prove that he was (Romans iv. 1-22). The explanation is that one intends to show that Abraham's faith was a working faith, and the other that faith alone availed to justify. In this sense approval can be given to the saying of an unknown author that "Good works are necessary to preserve a man in the state of justification, although they do not directly produce it", and also to the dictum of John Huss who said, "Where good works are not without, faith cannot be within".

Good works may therefore be said to be a source of comfort to the child of God. It is true that to regard good works in such a way as to put confidence in them, or to take comfort from them as a cause, is impossible; for no one can look upon anything he does with that boldness. No godly man ever satisfies his own heart in anything he does, much less can he satisfy the will of God. Nevertheless these good works, though imperfect, may be a great comfort to the child of God as the testimony of God's eternal love to him. The believer takes comfort from his good works, not to rest in them, but to find tokens of God's grace in his life.

In the third place, good works are necessary as the believer's testimony to others. The Lord said, "Let your light so shine before men, that they may see your good works, and glorify your Father which is in heaven" (Matthew v. 16). He does not here encourage vain-glory, but sets forth the true end of the believer's visible holiness. Godliness, being light, ought not to be placed under a bushel: it must be seen by others that thereby they may glorify God in heaven. As, when seeing an excellent picture, a man does not so much praise the picture as the artist who painted it, so those who perceive the godly life of the believer will be constrained to glorify God whose grace has transformed him.

Finally, good works are necessary as the believer's full salvation. A man's sins bring a twofold curse upon him: there is the guilt and there is the pollution. This means that salvation from sin will likewise be twofold; for if Christ redeems the believer from the guilt of his sins, He will also purify him from the contamination of them. Further, there is a consistency between deliverance from the power of sin in the present and deliverance from the presence of it in the future; in other words, there is a compatibility between good works and glory. Hence it is that, holiness having been appointed as the way, and salvation having been appointed as the end, there arises a relation between the one and the other. God has appointed the way of justification by faith, until, having brought the believer into eternal glory, He imparts perfect inherent holiness to him. In the glory the believer will be acceptable by reason of an inherent holiness wrought in him by the transforming grace of glorification. It was not impossible, of course, for God to have made him acceptable to Himself by the imparting of this perfect inherent holiness to him now, but in His wisdom God has chosen the way of justification by faith, that thereby the sinner might be humbled and His grace magnified.

It is possible to over-state the value of good works. Sometimes they are estimated too highly and given a kind of causality in justification and salvation which is quite contrary to the Divine purpose. This over-assessment of the value of good works is made more particularly in connection with faith, which, of course, is itself a spiritually good work; and claims are made for faith as a cause of justification which go far beyond the teaching of Scripture. Faith as a means of salvation is not introduced in the same sense in which works are rejected: it is not brought in as another form of good works as if in some oblique manner it were an efficient cause of salvation. It has its place in the salvation of a sinner only in the form of an instrumental cause, as the hand that stretches out to receive the gift.

Another view of the importance and value of good works is that, though they do not merit eternal life, for that is wholly purchased by Christ's death, yet godliness may procure certain degrees of glory. This can be taken as true, provided it is recognised that the rewards are rewards of grace; that is to say, though these rewards stand in some relation to good works, the meritorious cause of them is the enabling grace of God.

It is perhaps necessary to say at the end of a chapter of this kind that the fact that good works are necessary in the believer does not mean that the Covenant of Works is re-introduced, even in the modified form such as is found in the Arminian system of doctrine. Acceptance with God is not based on any willingness on God's part to accept a sincere though imperfect righteousness in lieu of perfect righteousness. The sinner is not pardoned for his past sin and then thrown back on his own best efforts to achieve his final and absolute justification. It cannot be too insistently reiterated that although good works are requisite in the justified or saved man, the basis of his acceptance is grace.

Let the believer, therefore, maintain good works,

and at the same time concur with Paul who said,
"By the grace of God I am what I am: and his grace
which was bestowed upon me was not in vain; but I
laboured more abundantly than they all: yet not I,
but the grace of God which was with me" (I Corinthians xv. 10).

CHAPTER V

THE LAW AND THE RIGHTEOUS MAN

In view of the goodness of the Law and the relation it bears to the glory of God and the good works of the believer, it is a little startling to come upon Paul's saying that "the law is not made for a righteous man" (I Timothy i. 9). The problem is not so great, however, as it might first appear. The difficulty resolves itself when it is remembered that Paul is not here undertaking a theological exposition of the use of the Law, but that he is simply making an observation which must be understood in relation to his immediate purpose. That immediate purpose seems to be to show that the primary aim of the Law is to deal with wrong-doing.

The crucial question that lies at the heart of some of the modern diversities of view about sanctification can be put as follows. Does the Law make active demands upon a man, commanding him and requiring obedience of him, or is it correct to think of the righteous man performing those things which are contained in the Law, but doing so without any awareness of the Law's active command? The question, therefore, would appear to be not whether the things of the Law are done by a believer, but whether, when these things are done, they are done by him as instructed and as commanded by the Law of God. The Antinomians of the seventeenth century were a little inconsistent, sometimes granting that the Law was a rule, and sometimes denying it to be so. They found difficulty in conceiving that Law should rule, if it did not also reign, by which they meant that if the law commands it must also, and of necessity, condemn. They therefore concluded it to be impossible that the condemning power of

the Law was inseparable from it. Their stock question was, "Can you put your conscience under the
mandatory, and yet keep it from the damnatory,
power of the Law?"

The antinomian argument, even in the present
day, is that a man is under either both of these
aspects of the Law or he is under neither. If a man
lives under commandment, it is said, he lives also
under condemnation; but, conversely, as the believer is not under condemnation so he is no longer
under commandment. This is a seriously mistaken
view and its weaknesses must be examined.

It may be conceded without question that a good
man feels no bondage by the Law, and indeed, often
acts rightly without conscious reference to the Law.
There is pleasure in obedience. Even secular writers, while making full acknowledgment of the value
of laws, nevertheless affirm that a good man does
what is right, not for fear of punishment, but for
love of righteousness. Thus Seneca says that it is
a poor thing to be good only according to the law,
and Aristotle shows how a righteous man would be
good even though there were no law, and Plato affirms that it is not fit to command or make laws
for those who are good. These sayings, of course,
are not the whole truth, nevertheless they have some
kind of truth in them. Similar views are expressed
by some of the early Christian writers. Jerome,
for example, asks, "What need has the Law to say
to a righteous man, 'Thou shalt not kill', when it
is not permitted to him even to be angry?" Chrysostom writes, "A righteous man does not need the
Law, nor does he require teaching or admonishing;
indeed, he disdains to be warned by it and he does
not wait or stay to learn of it. As therefore a mu-
sician or grammarian, who has these arts within
him, scorns the idea of consulting the rules or the
grammar, so does a righteous man." This, of

course, is very strong hyperbole and it must be cautiously understood; for what godly man is there who does not need the Law of God either as a light to guide him or as a goad to move him? It is no argument to say that in heaven the godly will not need the Law, for neither will they need the Gospel. Is it therefore to be concluded that the Gospel is of no use to them now? In the same way it is not to be assumed that the Law has no place in the life of the believer.

In what sense, then, does Paul teach that the Law is not made for a righteous man? There are three interpretations which come very near one another, all of which considerably help in understanding his meaning. One of them is that the Law is not a burden to the righteous man. This interpretation lays an emphasis on the word "made". It is not made as a burden to the godly man, but is a delight to him; he is not driven by the Law, but drawn by it. The righteous man is rather in the Law than under it, but as for the wicked his constant wish is that there were no Law.

Another interpretation is that Paul means that the Law does not condemn the righteous man. This refers the statement more particularly to the condemning aspect of the Law and understands the words to mean that the condemning power of the Law does not relate to the believer. This is what is indicated elsewhere by Paul when he says that the believer is not under the Law. It is, without doubt, true that the children of God are in themselves deserving of the curse of the Law, but by virtue of the sin-bearing death of Christ they do not experience its actual curse and condemnation. It does not therefore follow that there is no Law, because it does not curse; and so there is no necessary contradiction in saying that the Law can relate to the believer without condemning him.

A further interpretation is that the Law is not directed against the righteous man; that is to say, the Law was made not because of righteous men but because of those who were unrighteous. Had Adam continued in innocence there would not have been such a solemn declaration of the Law by Moses, for it would have been written in men's hearts. Therefore, though God gave a positive Law to Adam, for the testing of his obedience and the expression of his homage, yet He did not give it to him in this outward and formal way. Paul's phrase is therefore held to have a meaning rather like the proverb that says, "Good laws arise from evil manners"; and it is certainly true that laws, in the restraining and changing power they have upon the lives of men, are not for such who are already upright but for those who need to be made upright.

These interpretations receive some support in the Scripture. In the epistle to the Galatians Paul lists the virtues of godliness and then says, "against such there is no law" (Galatians v. 22, 23); by which he means that the Law was not made in respect of these things and has no condemnation of them. It is clear, however, that what is said of godly actions may be said of godly persons. Another passage bearing on this is found in the epistle to the Romans, "Rulers are not a terror to good works, but to the evil. Wilt thou then not be afraid of the power? do that which is good, and thou shalt have praise of the same" (Romans xiii. 3). Similarly, showing how dominated by love the Thessalonians were, Paul says, "As touching brotherly love ye need not that I write unto you: for ye yourselves are taught of God to love one another" (I Thessalonians iv. 9). His very saying, "Ye need not that I write", was itself a writing; so that his words mean no more than that the godly, so far as they are regenerate, delight in the Law of God and have no dread of it.

At this point there arises the danger of a false inference about the directing authority of the Law. The argument is made that because the believer delights to do what is good, therefore he does not need the Law to direct or regulate his behaviour. The fallacy of this inference can easily be seen in that it would follow equally as well that because faith is implanted in the believer's heart he does not need even the Gospel that calls upon him to believe. Historically, this false argument was taken up by some* who on the ground that the godly were made holy in themselves, denied that any part of the Scripture was needful to a man who had the Spirit. What the Antinomians restricted to the Law, as a "killing letter", these others applied to the whole Scripture; and, indeed, given the antinomian premiss, their argument is inescapable. Even in the earlier days of the Church there were not wanting those who fell into this mistake. Chrysostom, whose extravagance about the Law has been noted above, speaks in the same way about the Scriptures themselves and remarks, "We ought to have the word of God so engraved in our hearts, that there should be no need of Scripture", and Augustine tells of some who had attained to such holiness that they lived without a Bible. The obvious fallacy of such a conclusion as this proves the fallacy also of the premisses; that is to say, the completely erroneous nature of the antinomian opinion about the Law.

The Law has a directive power over a godly man for two reasons. The first of these has to do with directions for worship, an aspect of things that was a particularly sore point in the 17th century. It was argued that the true worship of God could not be distinguished from superstition and idolatry except by the First and Second Commandments. Many places in Scripture speak against false worship; but

* The Schwenkfeldians

the ability to discern what is false worship requires
the direction of the Second Commandment.

A second demonstration of the righteous man's
need of the Law arises from a comparison of the
height of the Law with the depth of sin. The standards of spirituality and holiness commanded in the
Law of God are far higher than ever a man can attain; therefore he is to study it more and more.
The psalmist prayed, "Open thou mine eyes, that
I may behold wondrous things out of thy law" (Psalm
cxix. 18), even though he was then a godly man and
his eyes had been in a great measure already opened
by the Spirit of God. As there is a height in the Law
so there is a depth in original sin; there is a great
deal more corruption in the heart of man than is
perceived by men, for "who can understand his
errors? Cleanse thou me from secret faults"
(Psalm xix. 12). There being such a world of corruption in the heart of man, there is all the greater
need of the spiritual and holy Law to make him see
himself thus polluted. So far as the believer is concerned, it cannot be doubted that part of his spiritual
growth is brought about by the very discovery of
the pride, the deadness and the uncleanness of his
heart of which he had no idea.

What, then, is the use of Paul's words about the
Law not being made for a righteous man? It is
clear that, when rightly understood, this passage is
to be used to stimulate the believer to pray for
such a love for God that the Law of God, far from
being a terror to his conscience, may be sweetness
and light. "Thy Law do I love", says the psalmist
(Psalm cxix. 113), and again, "My soul breaketh for
the longing that it hath unto thy judgments" (Psalm
cxix. 20); and Job says that he esteems the commandment more than his necessary food (Job xxiii.
12). Such must be the believer's filial affection to

God and His will, that he ought to love and delight
in His commandments, simply because they come
from Him. "Make me to go in the path of thy commandments; for therein do I delight" (Psalm cxix.
35).

CHAPTER VI

THE LAW WRITTEN IN THE HEART

The familiarity with the moral Law which is revealed in the consciences of all men everywhere has its explanation in the existence of natural Law. This concept of natural Law lies at the basis of the words of Paul who writes: "For when the Gentiles, which have not the law, do by nature the things contained in the law, these, having not the law, are a law unto themselves: which shew the work of the law written in their hearts" (Romans ii. 14, 15). The moral rule of God is one and the same everywhere and in all circumstances. There is thus a fundamental unity between the moral Law as formally promulgated in the Ten Commandments and that Law as it is found in the moral constitution of man. The extent of the knowledge of natural Law is as wide as the human race, for in Scripture the term "Gentile" usually signifies those who do not possess the Law of Moses. This is clearly Paul's meaning in the passage quoted above, for his purpose is to substantiate the charge which he brings against all mankind, both Jews and Gentiles, that by nature they are wholly in sin, and that God, being no respecter of persons, will judge the one as well as the other. Lest any should think that God's actions were unduly severe on the Gentiles, Paul establishes the truth that they too were not without some knowledge of His will, for the Law is "written in their hearts". By this phrase he draws attention to those survivals of the knowledge of God's Law which are found in natural reason and conscience. It is no contradiction to this that Paul also describes them as "having not the law". He means that they are without the Law in the sense of not having it in

the declared and publicly written form such as the
Jews possessed.

Three preliminary questions call for answer at
this stage. The first is, In what sense are the Gentiles said to do by nature the things of the Law?
These words obviously do not apply to all the masses
of the Gentiles, for Paul has already indicated in the
previous chapter that most of them lived in a complete disregard of the Law of God. Further, the
expression "things of the law" cannot refer to the
inwardness of the Law, but only to certain outward
acts which appear to conform to it. An unregenerate
man cannot do anything that is morally good, for
every moral action must have the glory of God as
its end, and at this the natural man does not aim.
The distinction that is sometimes made between
what is morally good and what is theologically good
cannot be substantiated, for every moral good ought
to be theological; that is to say, it must be good not
only in what is done, but in why it is done; not only
in its matter but in its motive. Because the unregenerate man fails in the qualifying motive he must
be said to be unable to do any work that is morally
good. It is also clear that, in saying that these external acts of Law-keeping were done "by nature",
the apostle means that they were performed by the
natural light of conscience.

The second question is, In what way may it be
said that the Law is "written in their hearts"? It
would be a mistake to identify this expression with
the promise given through Jeremiah, in which God
undertakes to write His Law in the hearts of His
people (Jeremiah xxxi. 33), for something far
greater than the merely natural is suggested by
these words. The writing of God's Law in the hearts
of men must therefore be recognised in a twofold
manner. The first form of writing has to do with
knowledge and reason, by means of which men are

endowed with an ability to discern good and evil; the second manner of writing has to do ·with the will and the affections and is found in the imparting to man of a delight in the Law of God and of the strength rightly to fulfil it. It is the former of these that is to be understood in Paul's words about the Gentiles.

The final question to be answered concerns the way in which the Gentiles reveal this Law written in their hearts. They do it in two ways. They show it outwardly by the way they make good laws and endeavour to live by them; and they reveal it inwardly in the quiet or disquiet of their consciences.

The evidence obtained in answer to these three questions provides the material for a searching challenge of the view that dismisses the Law from the life of the Christian. If there is a Law of nature written in men's hearts in this way, and if it continues to exert its authority with such persistence that a believer is bound to follow its direction; how can it be thought that the obligatory aspect of the moral Law can cease?

Attention has already been drawn to that denial of the continuing commanding power of the Law, which is based on the opinion that wherever the commanding act of the Law is, there also must be its condemning act. This is a fallacy, however, for it confuses the essence of the Law with what is only accidental to it. To command is of the essence of law, but to condemn is only accidental, being an effect of law which is contingent on the supposition of transgression. In the instance of the angels who never sinned, for example, the Law never exercised its condemning power; but it is perfectly plain that the angels were under its commanding power, because otherwise they could not have sinned, "for where no law is, there is no transgression" (Romans iv. 15).

The Law of Nature reveals itself in the common religious impressions which are found in all men everywhere. Like the first principles or axioms of science, no reason can be given for them: they are acknowledged to be self-evidencing.* It must be recognised, however, that the Law of Nature existed differently in Adam and in his posterity. In Adam it was perfectly known, but only a mere shadow of it is found in men today. The whole Law of Nature, containing perfect awareness of the will of God, was given to Adam at the first; and though there was the subsequent gift to him of a positive Law, to test his obedience, this in no way invalidated or detracted from the worth and significance of his original endowment with the Law of Nature. At the very beginning Adam was made after God's image, in righteousness and holiness; otherwise he would have been destitute of the light of reason and without a conscience.

What is covered by the Law of Nature is hard to determine, for what some have regarded as condemned by the Law of Nature others have thought to be approved by it. It has, accordingly, been defined in four ways. (a) It has been equated with those natural instincts in which man and beast agree, such as self-defence and desire of life; but this is plainly insufficient, for it would exclude such things as natural honesty and righteousness, for a beast is not capable of any sin or of obligation by a law. (b) It has been defined in terms of general custom; but this is so diversified that a sin with some is a

---

* Chrysostom remarks that when God forbad murder and such like, He gave no reason, because the prohibition was natural; but when He commanded the observance of the seventh day He gave a reason, namely, because on the seventh day the Lord rested. This, of course, does not imply that the commandment about the Sabbath is not moral: the difference is that the others are moral naturally and this one is moral positively.

virtue with others. (c) It has been regarded as co-extensive with reason in every man; but this, too, is most uncertain, for one man's reason is contrary to another's, and one man's conscience is more sensitive than another's. (d) It has been identified with the declared will of God; and this definition seems to be the most satisfactory.

The obligation of the Law of Nature derives from God who is the Author of it. It does not derive its binding power from its congruity with man's reason or conscience, but from the fact that it is the vice-regent of God and is a command from Him. It is therefore perpetual and can never be abrogated. This statement immediately raises the question whether or not the Law of Nature binds the Christian. Put another way, this is to ask, should a Christian listen to the voice of conscience? The answer must surely be that the Christian must refrain from committing an act of sin, not merely because of the intrinsic evil or circumstantial disadvantage of the thing, but also because the prohibition is within him in the form of the Law and command of God. There is no question, of course, that there is a difference between the form of the Law of Nature and that of the Ten Commandments; but they agree in this, that they are a rule of unchangeable and perpetual obligation. The Christian must not think that because Christ died to free him from the curse of the Law, that therefore he is freed from obedience to the Law of Nature as the very Law of God written within him.

The moral knowledge provided by the Law of Nature is sometimes called the light of nature, or natural reason. But this is a concept that needs to be used with care, for it is not difficult to see that though reason is necessary for man's knowledge of God, it is at the same time insufficient for all his spiritual needs. Reason does not by itself lead men to Christ.

Of the light of nature in fallen man there are three things to be said. In the first place, the light of nature must be regarded as a remnant of the image of God in man. However much it is rightly maintained that the image of God consisted primarily in righteousness and true holiness, it is equally true that, secondarily, it also included man's faculties as a rational creature. It is because of man's continued possession of the powers of reason that it may be said that the image of God still remains in him. Compared with faith, of course, the light of reason is exceedingly dim, yet there is some light still, and Paul has no hesitation in using the word "truth" to describe it (Romans i. 18). This moon-light, or glimmering, which reason provides has its use in the orderly conduct of society, in the stimulating of the practice of moral virtue, and in the removal of all excuse from those who do not glorify God according to the knowledge of Him which they have (Romans i. 20).

But, in the second place, the fact must not be ignored that the light of nature is obscured by sin. In the distortion of knowledge which sin has brought, the light of nature is not only of no help towards the things that are spiritually good, but is an enemy to them. The extraordinary situation thus comes about in which the more of natural reason there is in any particular opinion or action, the more opposition to God there is likely to be in it. This is how it was with all the great natural philosophers: they became vain in their reasonings; and the more they enquired and searched, the farther off they were from the truth (Romans i. 21, 22). "The natural man receiveth not the things of the Spirit of God: for they are foolishness unto him: neither can he know them, because they are spiritually discerned" (I Corinthians ii. 14).

In the third place, however, the light of nature is not to be summarily dismissed merely because it is weak, or because sin has now made it an enemy of God; for it is capable of being enlightened by the Word of God. When this Divine illumination is bestowed upon it the natural reason of man need not be despised or rejected. The relation between reason and faith has sometimes been compared with that between the poor soil at the root of a barren tree and the manure which the gardener uses. Let the soil first be taken out and the manure thrown in, then may the soil be replaced at the root of the tree, where it will now as much help the tree as it hindered it before. If reason be subordinated at first and the truth be received by faith, then reason may make full use of the truth, and this will be for the strengthening of the believer. So long therefore as the light of nature is not the rule, but is itself ruled and tested by God's Word, so long it cannot deceive.

The light of nature -- understood in the sense of being the remnant of the image of God in man -- is necessary in the religious and moral realm, in spite of its insufficiency; and this is shown in two directions. It is necessary first of all as a passive qualification in man as the subject of faith. An animal cannot exercise religious faith because it has no reason: it is reason, therefore, which puts man in a passive capacity to receive grace, even though he has no active ability for it. Secondly, it is necessary as an instrument of faith. A man cannot believe, unless he has some understanding or intelligence concerning what he is to believe. In Scripture, knowledge is sometimes put for faith because the one leads to the other reciprocally, and "through faith we understand" (Hebrews xi. 3). Reason is thus necessary as an instrument of faith.

A significant inference from the foregoing argument is that nothing can be true in Christian doctrine which contradicts the truth of God as found in the image of God in man. In the presence of such doctrines as the Trinity and the Incarnation -- doctrines which seem paradoxical to reason -- it may appear not easy to defend such a statement; yet, seeing the apostle calls the natural knowledge of a man "truth", and all truth is from God, by whatever means it comes, there can therefore be no ultimate contradiction between the truth acquired by nature and the truth given by revelation. The doctrines of the Trinity and the Incarnation must take their place among those things that are above reason but not by any means contradictory to it. It must also be observed that the same object may be known by the light of nature and by the light of faith. This may easily be exemplified: for a man by the light of nature may know that there is a God, and he may also believe it because the Scripture says so. Similarly, a man may by faith understand that the world was made (Hebrews xi. 3), and, at the same time, by reasoning he may know that it was made. Faith and the light of nature, therefore, contribute to the knowledge of the same thing in different ways: faith does it because of the testimony and revelation of God; and the light of nature does it because of reasons in the thing itself.

These two high claims for reason having been entered, a third observation must be made, namely, that although the light of nature is necessary it is not thereby a judge in matters of faith. Rationalism exalts reason too high, for it makes it not only an instrument but a judge, and thereupon rejects the greatest mysteries of the Gospel. The endeavour has many times been made to show that "religion is the highest reason", and there have been brilliant attempts to prove the truth of the Christian religion by reason; but it is impossible not to see how uncertain reason is in comparison with faith. Therefore, in giving a rightly important place to the understanding in the realm of spiritual things, care must be taken lest there be a confounding of the instrument and the judge: holy truths are Scripture truths, even though subsequently worked out by reason. The goldsmith takes gold plate and beats it into the shape he desires; nevertheless, his hammer does not make it gold, but only gold of such a shape. It is the same with the function of reason: it does not make a truth Divine, but only exhibits it and declares it to be so.

Closely linked with the Law written in the heart, yet widely distinct from it, are the commands of positive Law. Positive Law is met with in the very opening of human history in the words of God to the progenitors of the race, and they are recorded in the first book of the Bible. "But of the tree of the knowledge of good and evil, thou shalt not eat of it: for in the day that thou eatest thereof thou shalt surely die" (Genesis ii. 17). God's positive Law, here enunciated to Adam, is sometimes also called a symbolical commandment, because obedience to it was a symbol, or a sign, of man's homage and service to God. The object of this command was not something good or bad in its own nature, but something that was morally neutral or indifferent: it was evil, only because it was prohibited. The book of Genesis thus records that in addition to the natural Law written in man's heart, God also gave him a positive Law to put his obedience to the proof.

This positive Law consisted of the simple command to man to abstain from the fruit of the tree of the knowledge of good and evil. It is not easy to say why the tree was named in this manner, but

the interpretation which is the most usually received
is that the tree was so named, not from any of its
intrinsic effects, but from the historical event, that
is to say, because experientially it made Adam and
Eve to know good and evil.* This interpretation,
though good in itself, is not quite sufficient, for it
would seem that its name arose, not merely from
the historical event, but also by the decree and appointment of God. It was set before Adam to be a
kind of boundary and limit, that he should know that
good was what God permitted and evil was what God
forbad.

For what reason did God give man this positive
Law over and above the natural Law that was already in his heart? The first reason seems to be
that positive Law was instituted to draw man's attention to the fact of God's rightful dominion over
him. It is clear that to obey the natural Law might
be nothing more than a necessary condition of
existence and not in any way a true act of the will.
Some men, for example, abstain from certain sins,
not because they are forbidden by God, but because
their natural reason rejects them;** but these two
principles make the same actions to be totally different from each other. God purposed, therefore,
to try Adam by some positive Law, that in this way
the dominion which He had over him might be the
more clearly demonstrated. For this reason Adam
was not to consider the greatness or goodness of
what was commanded, but merely the will of Him who
gave him the commandment. Another reason, which

* This explanation is in harmony with what is a quite usual
feature in scripture, namely, the way of calling a thing by a
name which it had afterward.

** Even among Christians there is a great deal of difference
between good actions that are done because God commands and
those that are done because of natural reason.

follows from this, is that positive Law was given
in order that Adam's obedience might be the more
proved, and thus shown to be true obedience. By
means of such a commandment, the good of obedience in itself and the evil of disobedience in itself
was to be demonstrated. In passing, however, it
must be observed that though obedience to positive Law is far inferior to obedience to moral Law,
because the object of the latter is inwardly good
and the object of the former is rather a profession
of obedience than obedience, yet disobedience to
the positive Law is no less heinous than disobedience to the moral Law, because by this a man outwardly shows that he will not submit to God. It is
for this reason that Paul expressly calls Adam's
sin "disobedience" (Romans v. 19), not in the general
sense in which every sin is disobedience, but specif-
ically so, for, taken in the strict sense, his was
uniquely the sin of disobedience. By that act Adam
deliberately rejected the dominion that God had
over him; and though pride and unbelief were in
this sin, yet "disobedience" is what it properly was.

The positive Law given by God at this time must
be understood to have been universal; that is to say,
in being given to Adam, it was given to all the race
in him. This is why it is that Paul has to say that
all men sinned in the first man. The application of
this positive Law to Adam's descendants finds further proof, first of all, in the threat, "In the day
that thou eatest thereof thou shalt surely die" (Genesis ii. 17), and, then, in the subsequent event that
all the posterity of Adam has in fact died. In addition to this, of course, the same reasons which prove
a suitability of a positive Law in addition to the natural Law for Adam, hold likewise for the race des-
cended from him.

As clearly as the Law of God written in the
heart provides the basis of the congruity between

revelation and true reason, so also does positive
Law serve to establish the basis of the right of God
to command and the obligation of all men to obey.

CHAPTER VII

HUMAN ABILITY

It is very easy to go to extremes in assessing moral ability in fallen man: sometimes it is thought to be greater than it really is, and sometimes it is denied that there is any vestige of it remaining. There can be no doubt that man possesses the power of free-will, though when this is said it must be understood in regard to natural function and not to moral ability. Constituted as man is, with the endowments of personality, he has free-will, but since this is a power derived from and sustained by God, it is at all times dependent on God's help. So far as spiritually good things are concerned, the free-will of man has no ability at all, for the unrenewed man has no desire for such things and so cannot will them. Thus, while possessing a freedom which for the purposes of distinction may be called psychological, man is nevertheless a morally bound person: he is a slave to sin.

It is no contradiction of the foregoing to say that, despite all the corruption that is in man's heart, he may nevertheless do the outward form of the thing which is commanded by God and he may nominally abstain from what is prohibited. Because a man has the ability to conform to the Law in this outward way, he is thereby rendered inexcusable if he fails to do so. Man is able by the power of nature to refrain from many acts of gross sin, and, indeed, it must be regarded as one of God's mercies towards the human race that He has not abandoned man utterly.

Having acknowledged this about the natural power of men to perform external acts of obedience, it now needs to be said that everything they do is a sin before God. Whatever things unregenerate men do, though apparently glorious, they are but glorious sins, and the sinfulness of these things arises from a number of obvious reasons. Such works do not come from faith, or from one reconciled to God; and the person must be first accepted before the action. "Without faith it is impossible to please him" (Hebrews xi. 6). Such works do not come from a regenerate nature; and therefore the tree not being good, the fruit cannot be good. Such works cannot be acceptable to God, for they are not done for the right end. The unregenerate man is not able to do anything for the glory of God, for even his good deeds are but the casting out of one devil by another. Even if he intended some particular good end, such as to relieve the poor, this is not enough; for the ultimate and chief end must always be pursued, namely, the glory of God in all that he does.

The fact of human inability to do anything morally good raises a group of problems, and the first of these is whether the denial of man's power to do anything towards his salvation does not turn man into a mere stone or, at best, into some form of irrational creature. The answer, of course, is that this denial of human ability does nothing of the kind. The great and distinguishing thing about man is that in him there is the passive potentiality of conversion, even though there is no active power to turn himself to God. In distinction from the forces of nature and the irrational creatures, man is a being so made that he has, not merely a propensity, nor even a spontaneous inclination to do whatever actions are properly his own, but an inclination that belongs to the function of will. This, in turn, is accompanied by reason and judgment. Because man is thus constituted, the Divine work of conversion, though a work of new-creative power, is performed by means of arguments, or appeal to the mind. It is admitted that man has lost uprightness in mind and will, but he has not lost the faculties themselves; therefore, although he is spiritually dead to the things of God, yet he is volitionally alive and is a being capable of being influenced by arguments. The objection, therefore, may be granted that if a man had not this function of free-will there could be no conversion or obedience; for the work of God's Spirit is not to destroy man's nature but to perfect it.

The second problem raised by the fact of human inability is the seeming contradiction of pressing a duty upon man and at the same time acknowledging the gift of God's grace in the doing of it. In reply it must be said that if this is the dilemma of the theologian, it is first of all the dilemma of the Scriptures. This appears, for example, in the sermon of Christ delivered in the synagogue at Capernaum, where He says, "Labour not for the meat which perisheth, but for that meat which endureth" (John vi. 27); and yet at the same time declares, "No man can come to me except the Father which hath sent me draw him" (John vi. 44). The same appearance of contradiction occurs in the writings of Paul who says, "Work out your own salvation with fear and trembling. For it is God which worketh in you both to will and to do of his good pleasure" (Philippians ii. 12,13). The reason which the apostle gives in the second part would, according to the objection now being answered, quite overthrow the exhortation in the first. But to regard it as contradictory to press a duty and at the same time to acknowledge God's enabling in the doing of it, is to create a perpetual discord between commands and promises; for the same things which God commands the believer to do He also promises to do for him. Augustine replies to this problem with the exclamation, "O man, in God's precepts acknowledge what thou oughtest to do; in His promises acknowledge that thou canst not do it."

A third problem raised by the fact of human inability, and which is used as an argument against it, is that for God to command man is to mock him. It would be as if a blind man were commanded to see, or as if a man were told that if he would touch the sky with his finger he would receive a reward; and circumstantial and physical factors like this, it is held, would completely destroy the nature of a commandment. In reply to these objections, it must be observed that there are three ways in which a thing may be said to be impossible. (a) There is simple impossibility. All those things that involve a contradiction are logically impossible; and this impossibility arises from the nature of the thing. Such things are impossible even to the power of God, yet they do not signify any defect in Him. (b) There is natural impossibility. A thing may be impossible according to its nature, such as for a man to touch the sky or to work above natural causes. (c) There is moral impossibility. Things which have no simple or natural impossibility attaching to them sometimes become morally impossible through man's fault. It is no mockery for a man to do something which through his own fault he has made himself unable to do. If a creditor requires his debt of a bankrupt who has wastefully spent everything and made himself unable to pay, what unreasonableness is there is this requirement? It is, therefore, quite irrelevant to bring into the argument such impossibilities as asking men to touch the skies or of commanding blind men to see; for the impossibility under discussion is a moral one, and the impossibility to fulfil the commandment is an impossibility which man has brought upon himself.

A further problem in this connection attaches to

God's rebuke of man for his sins. It is sometimes asked, How can God reprove men for their transgressions if they can do no otherwise? But the answer to this comes from the same direction as that to the last question, for it still remains that whatever sin a man commits, it is properly his own fault and is truly his sin. Whatever that thing may be in which a man sins, he does it voluntarily and with great delight; and the more he delights in his sin, the more free he is in doing it. No man is ever forced to sin: he does it with all his inclination and desire.

In dealing with a fifth problem, it may be said to be beside the point to ask what purpose there is in exhortation and warning. For though God works every good thing in the believer, yet He does not do it upon him as if he were a stone; but He deals with a man suitably to his nature, that is to say, by means of arguments and reasons. If this is countered by saying that this is no more than to hold out a candle to a blind man, the further reply is that these exhortations, and the reading or preaching of the Word of God, are the instruments by which God will work these things. Preaching, therefore, must not be looked upon as if it were mere exhortation, but as a sanctified medium, or instrument, by which God works in man that to which He exhorts him. Preaching is the practical and operative means by which God effects His will in those who believe, even as when God said, "Let there be light: and there was light"; or when Christ said, "Lazarus, come forth. And he that was dead came forth" (Genesis i. 3; John xi. 43,44). The inworking grace of God in the believer does not supersede the necessity for exhortation.*

---

* This should keep men from despising even the most plain ministry or preaching; for a sermon does not work upon the

In solution of a further problem, it may be said that the acknowledgment of the necessity for the work of grace in the soul does not deny that the spiritual acts resulting are also truly and properly the believer's own. Reason and freedom qualify the sinner so that he is passively capable of grace: but when enabled by grace he is made active also. There is, indeed, no denying that to believe and to turn to God are acts of the sinner himself, for it is impossible to believe without the mind and the will: but this does not make man a joint-cause with God of his own salvation. It is incorrect to speak of the sinner as doing anything at all to procure his salvation, but at the same time he is active in receiving his salvation. Repentance and conversion and faith are truly the acts of the believer.

Finally, it must be affirmed that the sovereignty of God in His grace gives no support to a fatalistic attitude. It has sometimes been wrongly assumed that because salvation is all of grace and is sovereignly bestowed by God there is nothing for the sinner to do. In reply to this fatalistic point of view it is necessary to remember that there are two kinds of actions which, for the want of a better word, may be called holy: there are those that are inwardly and essentially so, and those which belong to the realm of outward actions. No man can do the former with God, but these outward actions such as hearing and reading God's word are within man's natural powers. God converts the sinner by the use of means. He does not work upon the heart as a craftsman uses an instrument; but He commands men to read and hear, and this is the means by which God will change their hearts. It is no excuse to say that even this reading and praying is sinful and

hearts of men on account of its elegance, but simply in so far as it is an instrument of God appointed to such an end.

therefore ought not to be indulged in; for man, sinner though he is, has the duty of praying to God and
seeking Him.

It will be seen, therefore, that no degree of human
inability to fulfil it can nullify the Law of God or in
any way reduce the authority of its claims.

CHAPTER VIII

THE MORAL LAW AND
ITS RELATION TO BELIEVERS

The controversy about the relation of the moral Law to believers centers in the Law given by God through the ministry of Moses to the people of Israel. What relation have believers to this Law of Moses? To answer this question it is first of all necessary to determine in what sense the word "law" is being used in such an expression as "the Law of Moses". Sometimes it is used in a wide sense and sometimes with a narrower meaning. It may be taken either for the whole dispensation and promulgation of the commandments, moral, judicial and ceremonial; or it may be employed more strictly for that part which is called the moral Law, together with the preface and the promises which are added to it; or it may be understood most strictly of all for that which consists in mere commandments, without any promise whatever. Most of the views which are held about the difference between the Law and the Gospel take the word Law in this last and strictest sense. But it is clear that if all the commandments and threatenings scattered up and down in the Scripture are taken to be properly the Law, and if all the gracious promises, wheresoever they are found, are then taken to be the Gospel, it will not be surprising that many hard things are said about the Law.

It has been customary to divide the body of the Mosaic laws into moral, ceremonial and judicial respectively, and though questions have been raised about this division, they are not of particular consequence, and the grouping may be safely accepted.

The portion of the Law of God with which the present study is concerned is the moral Law.

Not all the questions are answered, however, by the elimination of these other aspects of the Law of Moses, for the word "moral" has itself been used in a variety of senses. These different meanings have, in turn, provoked a number of further problems, not only in the exposition of the Law, but also in other aspects of Christian doctrine. The question demanding an answer therefore is what it is that makes a law moral. Although there is nothing in the connotation of the term to imply an obligation that is permanent, yet this is the meaning which belongs to the idea of moral Law; and it is this permanence of obligation which distinguishes that which is moral from those other obligations which are in other categories.

It is widely assumed that the Law of nature and the moral Law are identical; but this is a mistake, for there are at least two important differences between them. First of all, the moral Law given by God brings about a new obligation from the fact that it is formally commanded. Thus, although the substance of the Law of Nature and of the moral Law agree in many things, yet the man who breaks the Ten Commandments in their promulgated form is guilty of sinning more heinously than the man who has never received them. Secondly, although the moral Law requires many things which are also contained in the Law of nature, it also has far more in it than ever could be in that earlier Law. An example of this is to be found in the confession of Paul that he had not known lust to be sin unless the Law had said so, although he had the Law of nature to convince him of sin.

The moral Law was given to the people of Israel when they were in the wilderness at Mount Sinai, and there may perhaps be two reasons why at this

time, rather than sooner or later, God gave this
Law. The first reason was that the people of Israel
had fallen into idolatry, and so the Law was given
in order to restrain their idolatry and suppress
their rebellion. This would appear to be the meaning of the statement that the law "was added because
of transgressions" (Galatians iii. 19). The other,
and perhaps the most important, reason why God
gave the Law at this time, rather than another, was
that the Israelites were now becoming a nation.
They were about to enter into Canaan and to de-
velop a settled life, so God made laws for them;
for He was their King in a special manner, insomuch that all their laws, even political, were Divine.

It is a mistake to think of the moral Law as something new, for it is as original as the natural Law.
The moral Law existed long before the administration of it by Moses. Murder was a sin from the very
beginning, as appears by God's words to Cain; indeed, so also was the very anger itself that precedes
murder. Men, therefore, were never without the
Law, nor ever shall be, and there is a sense in
which it may truly be said that the Decalogue belongs to Adam, to Noah, to Abraham, to Christ, to
the Apostles, as well as to Moses. As has been
noticed above, there was, of course, a historical
reason why in the time of Moses there should be a
special promulgation and solemn repetition of it,
but even so the Law was perpetually heard among
men even from the very beginning. This consideration will greatly contribute to a right estimate of the
worth of the Law, it being the constant instrument
of God for the definition of man's duty, for conviction
of sin and for exhortation to holiness. To reject
the use of the Law, therefore, is to reject the universal way of God in both the Old and the New
Testaments.

The gift of the Law to Israel was an act of God's

infinite mercy and grace. In the addresses of Moses
to the people (Deuteronomy vii. and ix.), God im-
presses on the Israelites the greatness of His love
in giving them His commandments. He emphasises
again and again that it was not for their sakes, or
because of any merit in them, but purely because
He loved them. The psalmist takes up this goodness
of God in the giving of the Law by saying, "He hath
not dealt so with any nation" (Psalm cxlvii. 20), and
Hosea likewise stresses this mercy in the words,
"I have written to him the great things of my law"
(Hosea viii. 12). All the benefits that psalmists and
prophets regard as coming by the Law of God are
thus to be traced back to the grace and mercy of
God in giving the Law, and it is evidence of a deep
misconception of God's ways when the Law of God
is deprecated in any manner at all.

There is no disputing that, in the Gospel, God has
granted greater expressions of His love to man, but
this does not mean any diminishing of the grace that
is in the Law. The Law belongs to believers in the
present for the same evangelical ends as it was
originally given to the Israelites. Not one commandment can be read in its spiritual meaning -- which is
its true meaning -- without finding some cause to
praise God. It is not enough, therefore, that the
believer should not despise or neglect the Law: he
must the rather thank God that His Law is read
and expounded. Well may the godly man delight
to have that purity commanded which will make
him loathe himself, which will make him prize
Christ and grace the more, and which will be a
quick goad to all holiness. Besides all this, it is
false thinking even to contemplate a severance of
the Law from the Gospel, for when taken together
they mutually put a fresh relish and taste upon
each other.

A consideration of the majestic accompaniments

of the promulgation of the moral Law will serve
to exhibit its outstanding dignity. These accompaniments reveal that God put great glory on it; and
although the New Testament points out that the
Gospel ministration of grace is to be esteemed
more highly than the Mosaic ministration of it,
yet absolutely and in itself, the Law was greatly
honoured by God. It would be right to conclude that
God gave the Law in this solemn and impressive
manner in order that its authority and majesty might
be the more readily recognised. This dignity belongs peculiarly to the moral Law, in distinction
from the judicial and ceremonial; for although the
judicial and ceremonial Laws were given at the same
time as the moral Law, there is nevertheless a
great difference between them. It is recognised,
of course, that these three kinds of laws agree in
many particulars. They agree in their common efficient cause, which was God; they agree in the
minister or mediator, who was Moses; they agree
in the subject, which was the people of Israel; they
agree also in their common effects, which were to
bind the people to obedience and to punish those
who offended. But the moral Law is pre-eminent,
and this is seen firstly, in that it is the foundation
of the other Laws, and they are reduceable to it;
secondly, in that it is to abide always, whereas the
others were not; and thirdly, in that the moral Law
is distinguished from the others in having been
written by God, and in the command that it should
be kept in the ark.

Exception is sometimes taken to the relevance of
any discussion about the Law given by Moses, and
it is asked: Is the Christian a Jew? Does the Law
of Moses belong to believers? Has not Christ abolished the Law? Is not Moses, with his ministry,
now at an end? These are questions that are often
raised, and so it is worth enquiring whether the

Ten Commandments as given by Moses belong now to Christians or not.

It is needful, first of all, to investigate the sense in which it is said that the Law binds the believer in its Mosaic form. This is sometimes understood to mean that the Law binds because of Moses, so that whatever belongs to the Mosaic administration belongs also to the Christian. But such a view is false and is quite contrary to the whole current of Scripture; for then not only the moral Law, but also the ceremonial, would bind the Christian. Another way of understanding the relation to Moses is to say that it is purely on account of his having been the inspired writer. This, of course, cannot well be denied by any who hold that the Old Testament belongs to Christians; for why should not the books of Moses belong to them, as well as the books of the prophets? But there is a further way of understanding this relation of the believer to the Law of Moses. When God gave the Ten Commandments by Moses to the people of Israel, though they were the people to whom He then spoke, yet He intended the obligation to keep these commandments to fall not only upon the Israelites, but also upon all other peoples who in due time would be brought to a knowledge of Himself. The proper state of the question, then, is not whether Moses was a minister to Christians as well as to Israel (for that is clearly incorrect), but whether, when God delivered the Ten Commandments by the hand of Moses, He had in mind only the Israelites, or whether all other true worshippers of God were foreseen as included within their authority. This latter alternative is the true one, and at the same time defines the sense in which the Law binds the believer in its Mosaic form.

That this may be made more clear, it must be observed that the moral Law binds in two ways. It binds, first of all, in respect of its substance. To

the extent that much of this substance is found also
in the Law of Nature it applies universally, and so
was binding on the Israelites even before the promulgation of it on Mount Sinai. Secondly, it binds
in respect of the authority and command which are
put upon it; for when a Law is promulgated by a
proclamation, then an additional obligation comes
upon it. Thus when Moses as the servant of God
delivered this Law to Israel he thereby brought a
further obligation upon them. The main question to
be answered, however, is whether this obligation
was temporary or perpetual.

The chief problem is that of the perpetuity of the
Mosaic Law, and some light is given on this by
the fact of the revocation of that part of the Mosaic
Law which was purely ceremonial. It is obvious
that the obligatoriness of this ceremonial Law would
not have ceased unless the Law itself had been re-
voked; and so, by the same argument, the moral
Law given by Moses must still be binding unless it
can be shown that it is repealed.

Further, the ceremonial Law ceased, because it
contained but the shadows of the real, and when
Christ came there was no longer any need for the
shadows; similarly, the judicial Law ceased, because when the state of Israel came to an end there
was no more reason for the Laws. These Laws became obsolete by their very nature. No such thing
can be affirmed about the moral Law, however, for
the substance of that is perpetual, and there are no
places of Scripture which abrogate it.

The perpetuity of the Mosaic Law can be demonstrated by a number of arguments, the first of which
is an answer to an objection raised in connection
with the abolition of the ceremonial Law. It was the
apostolic opinion that, if the forms of ceremonial
worship were necessary for justification, this
would, in effect, either exclude Christ altogether,

or join Him together with the ceremonial Law.* It
is true that when the apostles demolish this error
they quite clearly show, not only that the works of
the ceremonial Law have no power to justify, but
also that the works of the moral Law are equally
unable to do this; but in acknowledging this fact, it
must be remembered that when the apostles bring
the moral Law into the dispute, they do it only in
respect of justification, and not in respect of obligation.

The second argument for the perpetuity of the
Mosaic Law is from the fact that the Scripture urges
the obligation of the moral Law upon converted Gentiles, and that this obligation is said to have come
down to them from their fathers, thus looking upon
Israelites and believing Gentiles as one people.
When Paul writes to the Romans he tells them that,
"Love is the fulfilling of the Law" (Romans xiii. 8,9);
and thereupon sums up the commandments which
were given by Moses. Similarly, when he writes
to the Gentile Ephesians, he urges children to hon-
our their father and mother because it is the first
commandment with promise: a commandment, of
course, which was entirely Mosaic in its source
(Ephesians vi. 2). This is further evident from the
epistle of James, which is to converted Gentiles as
well as to Jews. The words, "If ye fulfil the royal
law according to the scripture" (James ii. 8), are
an allusion, of course, to the Law of Moses, where
the second table contains love to one's neighbour;
and in the words, "He that said, Do not commit
adultery, said also, Do not kill" (James ii. 11), the
argument is drawn, not from the substance of the
Law, but from its Author, the God who spoke by
Moses. The reason why these commandments ex-
tend to the believing Gentiles is that the Jews and

* See Acts xv. 5,10,19,20,24,28,29.

believing Gentiles are looked upon as one people.
(See I Corinthians x. 1-2.)

The third argument is from the obligation upon
the Christian to keep the Sabbath day, an argument
that seems completely to confirm that the moral
Law given by Moses is binding upon Christians. If
the Sabbath day is a perpetual ordinance, and it is
based upon the fourth commandment, it cannot fail
to be seen that the commandments, as given by
Moses, are binding upon believers. The distinction
sometimes advanced concerning laws that bind "by
reason of the matter" and laws that bind "by reason
of the ministry" will not hold in this instance; for
the seventh day cannot bind from the matter of it,
there being nothing in nature why the seventh rather
than the fifth should oblige, but only from the mere
command of God for that day. If the Law of Moses
is disregarded in this respect, then, of course the
inference has to be made that Christians keep
the Sabbath day on New Testament grounds alone,
and not at all from the fourth commandment. This,
however, is at variance with the general consensus
of Christian thought, for all churches have honoured
the moral Law, together with its Preface, and have
it in their catechisms. It is not difficult, therefore,
to see that the distinction which affirms that the
moral Law binds as the Law of Nature, but not as
the Law of Moses, is untenable; for the Sabbath
Law, as it stands, cannot arise from the Law of
Nature, but has its morality and perpetuity from
the mere positive commandment of God.

The fourth argument is from reason, namely, that
it is incongruous to have a temporary obligation
upon a perpetual duty. It is wholly improbable that
God, when giving the Law by Moses, should have
intended that Law to be only temporary in its obligation, when the subject matter is in itself perpetual.
It is not a very reasonable supposition that the true

effect of the commandments should read, "You
shall have no other gods until after the time of
Moses", or, "You shall not murder or commit adultery while his ministry lasts, and then that obligation must cease and a new obligation come upon
you". Why should it be thought that, when the substance of the Law is necessary and perpetual, God
would alter and change the nature of the obligation?
Indeed, it is impossible to give even a remotely
probable reason for any such alteration.

The fifth argument for the perpetuity of the authority of the moral Law is that if the Law by the
hand of Moses does not bind the believer, then
the later books of the Old Testament do not belong
to him either, for they are basically -- especially
in their moral teaching -- nothing but expositions
of the moral Law. The rejection of the authority of
the Mosaic Law would carry with it the rejection
of the entire Old Testament.

There can be no flight from the claims of the
moral Law. Its demands belong to the very constitution of man as man, and are heightened by the
mercy of God that has reiterated His holy Law for
the salvation of sinners.

CHAPTER IX

THE SPIRITUALITY OF THE LAW
AND ITS USE
AS A MEANS OF CONVERSION

"Ye have heard that it was said by them of old
time ... But I say unto you" (Matthew v. 21,22).
These words refer to the teaching given by Moses
and the prophets in Old Testament times, and the
commandments which are quoted by Christ are
those of the Decalogue, but He gives a deeper sense
to them. Christ does not oppose the Law of Moses,
but only seeks to interpret that holy Law aright
and to remove from it the things that have defiled
and obscured it. That Christ does not give new
laws, but only interprets the old, is clear from
His words, "Think not that I am come to destroy
the law, or the prophets: I am not come to destroy,
but to fulfil" (Matthew v. 17). It is true, of course,
that Christ may be said to fulfil the Law in many
ways, but in the present context it would seem that,
as the contrast is between breaking the Law and
teaching the Law, Christ intends His hearers to
understand that He has not come to teach them
some new duty to which they were not obliged before, but that His purpose is to expound the Law to
them in such a way that they shall rightly understand
it and so become more conscious of their sin.

The very perfection of the Law serves also to
make it plain that it is impossible for Christ to have
added new duties, which were not commanded in
the Law. The Christian, therefore, is not to be
thought of as treading a more excellent way of duty
than that prescribed in the Law. There is no question, of course, that the Gospel goes far beyond the

Law in its remedy for sin, and also in its manifestation of God's grace; but on the subject of spiritual duties there cannot be a more excellent way of holiness than the Law, for it is the very idea and representation of the glorious nature of God.

Once more, that no additions to the Law are possible appears from the fact that its first part can be summed up in the requirement that a man should love God with all his heart and soul, and there can be nothing greater than this. Further, this command not only indicates the end to which the believer moves but also prescribes all the means which tend towards it.

Lastly, Christ does not say, "Except your righteousness exceed that of the Law of Moses", but "that of the Scribes and Pharisees", implying plainly that His intent is to expose their formal and hypocritical ways, and to show at the same time that they never understood the substance and excellence of the Law.

The reason why Christ needed to expound the Law in this way becomes evident as soon as the general view of the Jews about the commandments is considered. Their opinion was that the Law reached only to the outward man and prohibited only outward acts, and that even though a man cherished and purposed the outward acts of wrong-doing, yet so long as they were not outwardly committed there was no sin in him. This can be gathered from Paul who says that all the while he was influenced by these principles he did not understand inward lust to be sin. Christ's exposition of the Law is founded on the presupposition, first, that the Law is spiritual, and so forbids not only the fruit of sin, but even the root itself, and second, that wherever a sin is found to be forbidden, the contrary good thing is commanded. There need be no hesitation in preaching the Law as Christ here preaches it, for this is the efficient weapon to expose the formality and self-deception that are in the human heart.

The Law of God is such a perfect rule of life that Christ institutes no new duty which was not already commanded in that Law. As the exhortations of the prophets to faith and obedience were fundamentally an exposition of the Law, so also the commands of Christ and the apostles are but an urging of the things that are contained in the Law.*

It is true that in the Old Testament many things were expressed in a more material manner, and that the people for the most part understood them in this way; yet the duties then commanded were as spiritual as now. There is only a difference of grade in the manifestation of the duties, no specific difference of the duties themselves.

The excellence and spirituality of the Law is demonstrable from a large number of considerations. First of all, there can be no question that the Law of God required the worship and service of the heart. The Old Testament abounds in passages that call for the devotion of the heart, all of which are but an unfolding of what was implicit in the Law, and this spiritual quality is insisted upon in such a way as to make it plain that religious duties which were performed without the heart were not regarded by God. It is unhappily true that the people for the most part understood everything in a very poor way, thinking that only the outward duty was commanded. David, who may be taken as representing the truly godly persons of the Old Covenant, was acutely aware of his neglect of heart when

---

* This statement, of course, does not apply to the sacraments, or to the positive commands of outward worship, which are different from those ordained in the Old Testament, but to the moral duties required of men.

he prayed, "Unite my heart to fear thy name" (Psalm lxxxvi. 11).

Secondly, the Law of God laid greater stress on inward sanctification than on the external performances of religious works. This is frequently urged by the prophets, through whom God expresses His abhorrence of all the merely outward solemnities of His people, because they were not clean and pure in heart (Isaiah i. 10-20). David acknowledges, in the confession of his great sin, that a broken and a contrite heart is of more value than burnt-offerings (Psalm li. 16,17). This is a high concept, but the important thing to be observed just now is that it belongs to the Law of the Old Testament.

Thirdly, the Law of God required all duties to be done in faith and love. It is unthinkable that the requirements set forth in the first table of the Law, in which the people acknowledge Jehovah to be their God, should not include faith in Him as a God who was in covenant with them. How could the Israelites love God or pray to Him acceptably if they had not faith in Him? This demand for faith can be denied only if the Law is taken in so strict a manner that it includes nothing but commandments; but this would be a view of the Law such as is not usual. When the Law is seen in the context of its preface and the attached promises, it necessarily requires faith; for it is inconceivable that, when God commanded the people of Israel by Moses to worship Him and to acknowledge Him as their God, it was not His will also that they should believe in His love and care. Further, it has already been observed that love is commanded by the Law, for this is the manner in which Christ summarises it in both its parts. It is astonishing, therefore, that it could be thought that there was a contradiction between the doing of things in love and doing of them by the Law; for it is of the very substance of the Law that every command shall be fulfilled in love. It is true, of course, that the purpose of the Law was abused by Israel, and this led to bondage; but the Law itself was a call for love, and the more any Israelite did anything in love to God the more conformable he was to God's Law. The Law did not only require love to God, but commanded it in such a pre-eminent way that not even under the Gospel can anyone offer an expression of love higher than was then commanded. When Christ says, "He that loveth father or mother more than me is not worthy of me" (Matthew x. 37), He commands no higher thing of any Christian, than every Israelite was bound to do.[*]

Fourthly, another proof of the perfection of the Law can be seen in the spiritual motives which it required in man's approach to God. Sometimes the Israelites under the Old Covenant are looked upon as if they were completely bounded in their thought by earthly things; and it is assumed that the Israelites were moved in their religious duties only by material and temporal motives, and not by any spiritual considerations. That this is a quite false opinion can be seen by the protests of the prophets that when the people fasted, it was not to Him; and that when they complained, it was only because of their troubles and not because God was offended. In contrast with this mistaken view of a purely material motive in Old Testament worship, is to be placed the spiritual mourning of David as he cries, "Against thee, thee only, have I sinned" (Psalm li. 4), and the confession of Micah the prophet as he writes, "I will bear the indignation of the Lord, because I have sinned against him" (Micah vii. 9). What can be more spiritual than this?

---

[*] Note the commendation of Levi because in executing justice he knew neither "father" nor "mother".

Further, the Law of God required joy in God more
than in any created thing. This requirement was absolute, and the Gospel rises no higher in its demands. The language of the psalmist is as lofty as
any New Testament aspiration when he says, "Whom
have I in heaven but thee? and there is none upon
earth I desire beside thee" (Psalm lxxiii. 25). Did
he not esteem the Word of God above gold and
honey? (Psalm xix. 10) And when David was ban-
ished from his kingdom, it was not for a return to
that nor to any material good that he prayed, but
solely to see God in his beauty (Psalm xxvii. 4).
Thus, although the dispensation of the Law was not
so clear as the Gospel, yet those who were blessed
by God under it are found to have risen to equally
spiritual desires. The perfection called for by the
Law of God implies that its demands cannot be sur-
passed; for there cannot be a perfection that exceeds
perfection. The Law requires perfection of love
without defect of any kind; and so it is impossible
for any higher standards of holiness to be conceived
of than those contained within the Law.

A final evidence of the high spirituality of the Law
is to be found in the teaching of the Scripture that
the Law is designed for the purpose of grace. God
uses the Law as an instrument to stimulate holy and
spiritual desires in the believer. The Spirit of God
graciously inclines the heart and will of the believer
as the duties of the Law are pressed upon him, and
by this means Christ is so far from being excluded
that He is all the more glorified and honoured.*

---

* The perfection of the Law has been many times challenged,
and the view is held by some that Christ delivered better precepts than those of Moses, therefore He is to be recognised not
so much as an interpreter as a reformer. It is, of course, quite
understandable how some may be led into this erroneous opinion, because Christ's interpretations are so high and glorious;
but it is nevertheless incorrect to say that He brought command-

The acknowledgment of the high and spiritual demands of the Law leads to the recognition of the place of the Law as a means of conversion. This is sometimes denied by the counter-argument that the only instrument designed for this end is the Gospel. There is obviously no need to plead that the Gospel is an instrument for the conversion of men, for all acknowledge that, but in the presence of opinions to the contrary it would appear to be necessary to maintain the other equally Divine truth that the preaching of the Law of God may be blessed by Him to bring about the conversion of men. It is of importance to establish this doctrine; for if the contrary were true, it would be the preacher's duty in great measure to lay aside the preaching of the moral Law, as not instrumental or subservient to that main end of the ministry, which is the conversion of sinners.

In the consideration of the instrumental value of the preaching of the Law for the conversion of sinners there are three things to be premised. The first is that the Law could never be instrumental to the regeneration of men were it not for the Gospel promise. If God had not mercifully promised to give a new heart through Christ, there would have been no way to make anything effectual that is preached out of the Law; so that, for instance, while a preacher, speaking on the commandments, is instrumental

---

ments of another kind than those contained in the Law of Moses. The instance brought forward in favour of the view that Christ introduced new commandments is, among others, that concerning the law of swearing. It is a mistake to think that Christ made swearing absolutely unlawful, for here, too, is a clear case of that removal by Christ of those corrupt glosses with which the Law had been overlaid by the Pharisees. The same is true about the difficult problems of capital punishment, of war, of litigation and of revenge.

in changing the hearts of his hearers, all this benefit must be acknowledged to have come by Christ,
who died, rise again and ascended into heaven in
order that the things so preached might be effective
in the salvation of men. The truth is that there
never was in the Church of God "mere pure Law"
or "mere pure Gospel"; but they have ever been
subservient to each other in the great work of conversion. The question, then, is not whether converting grace is inherent in the Law as such, but whether
converting grace operates along with the preaching
of the Law. The concern of the present argument is
not to define the difference between the Law and the
Gospel -- a difference which is admitted by all -- but
to affirm that God may make the exposition of the
moral Law to be an instrument for a man's conversion.

The second thing to be premised is that although
the preaching of the Law may be blessed to the conversion of the sinner, yet the substance of the Law
is never itself the ground of justification. This
means that when a man repents and turns to God
from his sins, he cannot have hope of acceptance
in anything he does, but it must be solely in the
promise of the Gospel.* There must on the one hand
be no confounding of the Law and Gospel, nor yet,
on the other, may they be made so contrary in their
nature and effect that where one is the other cannot
be.

The third premiss is that the Law of God, being

---

⁴ * The difference between the Law and the Gospel, therefore,
does not lie, as is sometimes affirmed, in that one is the instrument of grace and the other is not; but in this, that a sinner is
not justified on the grounds of any holiness brought about in himself (by the preaching of either Law or Gospel), but in an
entirely evangelical manner; that is, by God's forgiveness of
whatever is sinful and by the imputation of the righteousness
of Christ.

part of God's Word, is as much the instrument of conversion as is the rest of that Word. The commandments are not only informative of duty, but are practical and operative means appointed by God to work that which is commanded.

When the use of the Law in the conversion of sinners is recognised, it still needs to be asked whether the Law can be effectual entirely of itself or whether the result is really the work of the Spirit in the sinner by means of the Law. In answer to this, and in general substantiation of what has already been said, the following observations must be made. In the first place, the Word of God as it is read or preached, if considered in itself alone, works only in an objective manner towards the conversion of a man. Taken in itself, as not animated by the Spirit of God, the utmost it can do is to present itself as an object of understanding. Apart from the application of the truth by the Spirit of God, the Word can effect no regeneration of the heart. If the Spirit of God be taken away from the Word, then the whole Scripture is a "killing letter", even that part of it which is called the Gospel. The promises of the Gospel may be preached a thousand times over, but they convey no grace if the Spirit of God be not there effectually.

It follows from this in the second place, that whatever blessings come to the soul by the preaching of either the Law or the Gospel are brought about efficiently by God's Spirit. For this reason, it may sometimes be that the Law is more effective than the Gospel for the awakening and conversion of a sinner. It is not impossible to suppose a preaching of the Law accompanied by the Spirit of God in such a way as to change the heart of a man: and similarly it is not impossible to suppose a preaching of the Gospel in the greatest glory of it, yet, it being not accompanied by God's Spirit, there may not be the least degree of grace accomplished in any hearer. It is therefore quite superficial to say that the Law shows a man his duty, but the Gospel gives him grace to do it; for how many there are who hear the promises of the Gospel but who nevertheless receive no benefit from them? Conversely, however, if the Law, which sets forth the duty of man, is accompanied by the power of God's Spirit, it may well instrumentally work in man an ability to do it. That the Scripture without the Spirit of God cannot convert a sinner is plain, for if it could, then the devils and men of intellectual powers, who understand the letter of the Scripture better than others, would be sooner converted; hence the Word of God, even though it is spoken of as a sword, is nevertheless called "the sword of the Spirit" (Ephesians vi. 17).

The foregoing premises having been laid down, the arguments which prove the preaching of the Law to be a means of conversion must now be presented. It is clear, first of all, that whatever is attributed to the whole ought not to be denied to the part. It is the property of the whole Word of God to be the instrument of conversion; and therefore this must not be denied in respect to the Law. But, further, the Law is expressly said to be instrumental in the work of conversion. The Law is called spiritual (Romans vii. 14) because it is that which works spiritually in the heart of man; and the psalmist writes, "The law of the Lord is perfect, converting the soul" (Psalm xix. 7). Can it be thought that when the psalmist commends the Law of the Lord in this way, that he means all the Word of God except the moral Law, when indeed that was the greatest part of it in his time?

An even stronger evidence for the use of the Law in the conversion of sinners is found in the fact that Christ used the Law for this purpose. To hold that the preaching of the Law is not a means to conversion must imply that Christ did not take the most direct way to convert His hearers in the Sermon on the Mount, for if that sermon be considered it will be found that it is principally occupied with the exposition of the moral Law and the pressing of its duties. How can it be thought otherwise than that the Lord judged this to be profitable and soul-saving material?

It must be obvious also that the objective nature of the Law fits it as an instrument for conversion. It is when the purity and excellence of the substance of the Law are proclaimed that the Spirit of God, by the use of that holy Law, moves the heart of man to love it. If the philosopher said of virtue that if it could be seen with bodily eyes the beauty of it would ravish men: how much more may this be true of the purity and holiness of the Law.

Finally, it cannot be that the moral Law should come behind the ceremonial in its usefulness. If the ceremonial Law, with its sacrifices, was blessed by God's Spirit during the period of its use, notwithstanding the fact that its institutions are now obsolete, then may also the moral Law be blessed by God for spiritual effects, seeing it still stands in force.

This chapter may be concluded by an appeal to experience which, though not itself an authoritative foundation for argument, nevertheless bears testimony to the truth that God uses His holy Law to bring sinners to themselves and thus to Himself.

CHAPTER X

THE LAW NOT ABROGATED BY CHRIST
TO BELIEVERS

The basic question of the historic antinomian controversy was whether or not the moral Law of God is abrogated in the Gospel; and it was the assertion that it is thus abrogated which gave Antinomianism its name. This issue is presenting itself again in connection with some of the current and popular expositions of the doctrine of sanctification.

The answer to the question about the abrogation of the Law is given categorically by Paul when he writes, "Do we then make void the law through faith? God forbid: yea, we establish the law" (Romans iii. 31). In the preceding verses he lays down the nature of justification so exactly that all the causes -- efficient, meritorious, formal, instrumental, and final -- are clearly described, as also is the consequent of this truth, namely, the excluding of all self-confidence and boasting in what a man does. He then draws a conclusion which he states both positively and negatively (Romans iii. 28). The positive statement is that justification is "by faith"; the negative statement is that it is "without the deeds of the law". When all this is said, the apostle brings forward an objection in order to refute the charge that he was destroying the Law. He asks, "Do we make void the Law?"* The only reply which the apostle makes to this is an ejaculation of abhorrence, "God forbid", by which strong expression it is clear how intolerable such a doctrine ought to

* The word employed by the apostle was previously used by him in ver. 3 and means to make "empty" and of "no effect".

be. Paul not only repudiates the insinuation that
he is destroying the Law, but substitutes an assertion in its place. He adds, "Yea, we establish the
law", using a metaphor from the strengthening of
some structure that was likely to fall.

Many interpreters have been perplexed that Paul
can thus say that he establishes the Law, especially
considering those many places in his epistles which
seem to abrogate it. One suggestion is that Paul
means no more than that the Law is now established in the sense that the truth to which it bore
witness has now come to pass. (See ver. 21.) This
interpretation, however, is plainly insufficient.
Another suggestion, based on the view that these
words refer to the ceremonial Law, finds their
meaning in the fact that the ceremonies and types
were fulfilled in Christ. This, again, is not quite
adequate, for when the apostle speaks about the
Law in this place he most certainly includes the
Moral Law.

The Law is established by the Gospel in three
ways. Firstly, in respect of its penalties: this aspect was established in Christ, who satisfied the
justice of God. Secondly, in respect of its requirement of perfect obedience: this also was fulfilled
in Christ.* Thirdly, and what seems to be Paul's
chief purpose in this passage, the Law is established
by the Gospel because the believer obtains grace in
some measure to fulfil the Law. The believer thus
still keeps the Law in its preceptive part, and by
faith in Christ is helped to a life of obedience to it.

---

* It is a question worth pursuing, whether the righteousness
by which a believer is justified is in any way the righteousness of
the Law. Within the right understanding of the terms employed
there can be no hesitation in affirming that this is so. The
doctrine of the imputation of Christ's active obedience to the
believer is beyond all doubt an establishing of the Law in this
manner.

The truth which emerges from a right understanding of Paul's words in this passage is, therefore, that the doctrine of grace, when seen at its heighest and fullest, does not overthrow the Law, but rather establishes it.

There is, nevertheless, a further question to be discussed, namely, whether Christ, having established the Law in the manner already observed, then abrogated it so far as its authority over the believer is concerned. It would seem at first as if the Scripture contains some contradictions on this subject. For example, in the passage under examination Paul denies that his teachings "make void the law"; yet in another passage he expressly uses the word* which is here denied and speaks of the Law as "that which is done away" (II Corinthians iii. 1).

There is no abrogation of the Law in the Gospel. A careful distinction must be made between the abrogation of a law and its relaxation. Relaxation supposes a law still standing in force, but abrogation means that a law is totally taken away. Such abrogation arises sometimes from the original constitution of the law, which limited and prescribed the time for which it should continue; and sometimes it arises from an explicit revocation of the law by that authority which made it. It may be easily proved that there has been an abrogation of the ceremonial and judicial laws; but there is no such abrogation of the moral Law. It is true, of course, that there is some mitigation of the severe application of the Law in respect of the person of the believer; but this is not an abrogation of the Law, for Christ vindicated the Law on the sinner's behalf and bore its curse as the sinner's Surety. The change that comes about through the grace of God

* The word is καταργέω

is not a change in the Law, but a change in the sinner towards the Law.

Closer attention, however, has still to be paid to the concept of the Law as a covenant. The covenant of Law is now ended, but the rule of Law is eternal. There is some difference of judgment among expositors about the nature of the covenant of Law. Some make the Law a Covenant of Works and hold that it is upon the ground that its covenant aspect is ended; others call it a subservient covenant to the Covenant of Grace, and regard it as introduced only to enhance the glory of God's grace; there is a third group who call the covenant of Law a mixed covenant of works and grace, but this can scarcely be comprehended as possible, much less as true. The view which seems most likely to be correct is the one which understands that since the Fall God never entered into covenant with man on any other basis than that of grace, and that therefore the Law given by Moses was itself part of the Covenant of Grace. The covenant of Law, even as an expression of the Covenant of Grace, is brought to an end because though the essence of the former covenant and that of the one that replaced it are the same, yet the administration of the former is altogether outmoded.* It is perfectly clear, therefore, that whoever looks to the Law for life and justification abuses the Law and turns it into a man made covenant of works.

One of the attempts to expel the Law of God from the life of the believer is based upon the illogical assertion that the Law as such is abolished but its substance remains obligatory. But how can obligation be present without the presence also of that which is essentially law? Law and obligation imply each other. For if the continuing substance of the Law carries obligation with it, then when a believer

* This appears from Hebrews vii. 18,19 and viii. 7,8.

does not walk according to his duty he sins. Not to comply with the obligation is not to comply with the Law. Again, to say that the matter of the Law binds, but yet not as a law, is a contradiction in terms; for what is a law if it is not something laid down by the command and will of a superior? If this be pressed to a particular application, it may be asked whether love for God, which is the substance of the Law, is not also the will of God. It would seem to be illogical to assert that love to God should bind believers merely because the matter itself is good, but that it should not on any account bind them because God wills them to love Him. Furthermore, views which deprecate the Law of God must necessarily deny not only the obligatory nature of the Law, but even the will of God in requiring believers to love Him; for a law is nothing but the will of the Law-giver.

The premise which asserts the abrogation of the Law to the believer quickly leads to an impossible conclusion, for if the Law is abrogated to believers under the New Covenant it must be regarded as equally abrogated to believers under the Old. There is no half-way position in this argument, for either it must be denied that there were any believers under the Old Covenant, or, if there were, then they were freed from the Law as much as believers are now. If the Law be taken for the entire administration of the Old Covenant then, of course, believers under the Gospel are free from it in such a way that believers of earlier times were not: but if the Law be understood in respect of its essential parts in directing and commanding, then these things are either still equally in force, or else equally abrogated to all believers, whether under the Old Covenant or the New. The arguments against the subjection of believers to the Law under the New

Covenant are equally as strong against the subjection of those who were under the Old.

From some points of view it is possible to make what might be called concessions to the idea of the abrogation of the Law, but it cannot be insisted upon too strongly that in the proper sense of the word there is no abrogation whatsoever. The concession may be made in a purely verbal respect because so many reformed theologians have spoken of the abrogation of the Law, though not with that erroneous meaning attaching to the word which is here being refuted. In a loose way of speaking it may also be conceded that there is an abrogation of the Law to believers in respect of justification, but, strictly the Law was never designed by God to be an instrument of justification, and so it is not properly relevant to speak even of the mitigation of the Law. In fact, in all aspects of salvation, if the Law is "established" as the apostle says, then there can be no talk of its "abrogation". The far better word, therefore, is mitigation.

It is when the believer's walk with God is considered that some mitigation of the Law may be acknowledged. The believer is freed, for example, from the burdensomeness of a rigid obedience, though there must be no misunderstanding here, for the deliverance of Christ is not of such a sort that the believer is no longer under obligation to render a perfect obedience. It must be maintained that for the believer not to obey the Law of God to its utmost perfection is a sin, and that every believer sins in this respect; nevertheless, such is the mercy of God in Christ that the believer's obedience to the Law, which is but inchoate and imperfect, is accepted by God through the merits of Christ. This is a mitigation which arises solely from the fact of grace in Christ, for the Law, strictly taken, would still condemn the sinner.

This mitigation may also be seen in respect of
the way in which the Law no longer provokes sin
in the believer as it does in the unbeliever. In the
Epistle to the Romans the apostle complained that
the Law of God had the bitter effect of making him
the worse (Romans vii. 8). The more spiritual and
supernatural the Law was, the more his carnal and
corrupt heart resented it: so that the more the Law
would dam up the torrent of sinful lusts, the higher
they rose. But this painful experience is not to be
ascribed to the Law, but to Paul's corruption. It is
not the brightness of light that dims the sight or
blinds the eyes, for light was especially created
by God for them, but the infirmity and weakness of
the eyes, which are not able to endure such brightness. The experience of the Law in the heart of the
believer may be illustrated from nature. As the
thorns that are cut down sprout again even more
abundantly, so do corruptions while cut off by the
Law, because they remain fixed and rooted in
the sinner's heart. In the godly, however, because
there is a new nature and a principle of love and
delight in the Law of God created within him, his
corruption does not increase and grow by the Law
but is rather subdued and qualled. The provocative
power of the Law is thus mitigated by the effect of
grace within the heart.*

Although the Law is mitigated or relaxed in relation to believers in the ways now noticed, it must
nevertheless be affirmed that the Law perpetually
continues as a rule of life to them. In support of
this it must be observed, first of all, that the different phrases that the Scripture uses concerning

Ч * In the experience of the wholly unregenerate, it should be
noted, it is not only the commandment of the Law that stirs up
evil in his heart, but also the promises of the Gospel. The difference of effect depends, therefore, on the difference in the
persons.

the ceremonial Law and its abrogation* are no-
where applied to the moral Law. It has never been
said of the moral Law, that it is changed, or becomes old, or is abrogated, which expressions
denote a change in the Law; but when the Scripture
speaks of the moral Law it says that the believer
is "dead" to it and that he is "redeemed" from the
curse of it, which phrases imply that the change
is in the believer and not in the Law.

A second consideration is that the holiness required of the believer is nothing but conformity
to the Law. It is perfectly clear that when the
apostle spoke against the Law, he was not speaking
of it as the rule which obliges the believer to its
obedience. For example, in writing to the Galatians,
he plainly warns those who desire to be justified
by the Law of their hopeless condition (Galatians
v. 4), but he immediately proceeds to urge them not
to use the liberty which Christ gives as an occasion
to the flesh, and he gives this reason, "For all the
law is fulfilled in one word, even in this, Thou shalt
love thy neighbour as thyself" (Galatians v. 14). Is
the apostle contradicting himself in the same chapter? Is he urging them to obey the Law and yet at
the same time reproving them for desiring to be
under it? Certainly not; the circumstances were
different. When they desire to seek justification
by the Law, then he warns them; but when they are
neglectful of their obligation to obey the Law, then
he rebukes them.

Further, disobedience to the Law is still a sin
in the believer. If there is sin there must also be
Law, for sin is transgression of a law (I John iii. 4).
When David commits adultery, or when Peter denies
Christ, are not these sins in them? If so, is not
David's adultery a sin because it is against a

---

* See Ephesians ii. 14,15; Hebrews vii. 12,18 and viii. 13.

particular commandment? It is an evasion to say that
it is a sin only against the love of Christ, for then
there would be no sins but sins of unkindness or
unthankfulness. Christ's love may indeed be the
supreme reason for obeying the commands of God,
but that does not hinder the command itself from
binding the believer as the expression of the will
of the Law-giver.

Finally, it is obvious that there are many reasons
why the ceremonial Law should be abrogated which
can in no way apply to the moral. In the first place
the object of the ceremonial Law was not something
perpetual, nor was it in itself true holiness. To
circumcise and to offer sacrifices were not in themselves holy and good, nor is the leaving of them a
sin; whereas the matter of the moral Law is perpetually good, and failure to perform it is necessarily
a sin. Can it be thought that it was all the same to
God whether a man was an adulterer or chaste, as
it was whether a man was circumcised or not circumcised? Again, the ceremonial Law was typical
and foreshadowed Christ who was to come; but now
that He is come there is no use for these ceremonies. Lastly, the Jews and the Gentiles were to
be joined into one body, with no difference between
them; and to effect this it was necessary that the
partition-wall of ceremonies should be pulled down;
but no such circumstance affects the permanence of
the moral Law.

It is necessary to pay some attention to those
Scriptures which seem to indicate that the moral
Law was to endure for a limited time only and in
the same manner as the ceremonial Law. The first
of these for consideration is the statement, "The law
and the prophets were until John",* words which
are sometimes understood to mean that the Law

* Luke xvi. 16, and see also Matthew xi. 13.

was to continue only until John's time. This passage,
of course, provides no proof at all that the Law was
to be abrogated when John the Baptist came; for,
lest any should misunderstand His words in such a
way the Lord immediately adds, "It is easier for
heaven and earth to pass, than one tittle of the law
to fail" (Luke xvi. 17). The meaning, therefore, is
that the Law was to cease in so far as it prefigured
Christ, that is to say, in its ceremonial and typical
aspect. For this reason the Law and the prophets
are put together, as agreeing in one general thing,
namely, to foretell of Christ and to typify Him.

The next Scripture to be considered is that well-
known sentence so much used in this controversy,
which reads, "For ye are not under the law, but
under grace" (Romans vi. 14). For the exposition
of these words it must be asked in what sense Paul
is arguing against the Law and what is the proper
subject under discussion. This inquiry runs back
to the question raised by some believing Pharisees
in Jerusalem who so pressed the necessity of
circumcision that they joined Moses and Christ together (Acts xv). It seems that in spite of the de-
cision of the council which condemned that opinion,
there were nevertheless many who persisted in requiring circumcision, and this, in turn, necessitated
the refutation by the apostle of such a false view
of the Gospel. As has been observed in an earlier
chapter in this discussion, although the keeping of
the ceremonial Law was the occasion of the controversy in the first place, yet Paul now extends his
arguments to include the moral Law, because of
the widespread assumption among the Jews that
the observance of the moral Law without Christ
was enough for their salvation. It is plain, however,
that the apostle is arguing against the Law not in
its own nature and glory, but only in the Jewish
abuse of it. The argument transferred itself, as it

were, from the ceremonial Law to the moral Law
because of the false reasoning of the Jews. If the
Jews could persuade themselves that the external
performance of the ceremonial Law was enough to
make them acceptable with God, even though they
lived in gross disobedience to the moral Law, how
much more would they deceive themselves about
their acceptance with God when they lived a life
externally conformable to the moral Law! It is in
a context of this kind that the apostle seems to speak
things derogatory to the Law, because the Jews
took it without Christ; just as he likewise calls the
ceremonies beggarly elements, when he knew, of
course, that they were signs of an evangelical grace.

It is extremely important to observe that the
apostle uses the word "law" in different senses,
because failure to discern these differences has
been the occasion of much misunderstanding. In
most of the passages where the Law seems to be
abolished, it is taken in one of two senses. Sometimes it is used synecdochically, in which the whole
is put for part, that is to say, the word Law has
been used for only that part which condemns. An
example of this is the passage where the apostle
says, "Against such there is no law" (Galatians
v. 23), and speaks as if there were nothing in a law
but condemnation. On other occasions the word
"law" is put for the ministry of Moses, as a dispensation that was far inferior to the ministry of
the Gospel (See Galatians iv. 25, v. 1-4). Before any
conclusions are drawn, therefore, about Paul's view
of the abolition of the Law, the first task is that of
defining the sense in which the term is being employed.

Another important task in this respect is to determine the different meanings of such phrases as,
"without the law", "in the law", "of the law", and

"under the law". "Without the law" is to be understood in two ways: first, a man is "without the law",
in the sense of being without the knowledge of it;
thus the Gentiles are "without the law" (Romans
ii. 12); and second, a man is "without the law" when
he is without the experience of the accusing and
terrifying power of the Law (Romans vii. 9). Opposite to the phrase "without the law", is the expression "in the law" (Romans ii. 12), and in this passage
it signifies those who possess the knowledge of the
Law and yet sin against it. Much to the same purpose is the phrase "of the law" (Romans iv. 14)
which sometimes is equivalent to "of the circumcision" (Colossians iv. 11; Titus i. 10), namely,
those who are initiated into the ministry of Moses.
The apostle uses also another phrase, "by the law"
(Galatians ii. 21), meaning by works done in conformity to the Law; and it is in this sense that the
apostle urges that righteousness is not "by the law".
All the difficulty in the present controversy, however, is about the phrase, "under the law", and it is
to this that special attention has to be given.

It is, of course, possible for a believer to put
himself "under the law" in a voluntary manner.
Christ put Himself under the Law in this way, and
so also did Paul. The apostle refers to this when
he says that he become to some "as under the law"
(I Corinthians ix. 20), though in this case it was the
ceremonial Law under which he was prepared to
place himself. Paul also describes himself as "in
the law to Christ" (ἔννομος), for though a godly
man is not properly "under the Law" (ὑπό νόμου),
he is nevertheless "in the law" (ἔννομος), and he
adds the words "to Christ", however, so that none
should think that he spoke of the whole Law, in-
cluding the ceremonial part of it which was abolished
by Christ. In this well-explained sense, then a godly
man may be said to be under the Law.

How far may the phrase "not under the law" and "not under the curse" be equated? There is one sense in which they might appear to have the same meaning, as in the question, "Shall we sin, because we are not under the law, but under grace?" (Romans vi. 15) Because Paul is here speaking of sanctification, however, both in this chapter and the chapter following, it seems preferable to make the phrase "under the law" to mean the same thing as the phrase "under sin"; for the apostle, speaking of himself as carnal, says that the Law wrought in him all manner of evil (Romans vii. 8). This, indeed, is the work of the Law in every unregenerate man; so that the more the Law is applied to him the more does his corruption break out. The apostle's argument, then, is this: "Let not sin reign in you, for now you are not under the Law stirring up sin and provoking it in you, but under sanctifying and healing grace".

The third passage that seems to teach that the moral Law was to endure for a limited time only is that in which Paul says, "Ye also are become dead to the law" (Romans vii. 4). The apostle explains what it is to be under the Law by an analogy from a married woman who is bound to her husband as long as he lives, but who, when her husband dies, is free. In the exposition of this analogy there is some difference among commentators, but the following seems to be the meaning. The former "husband" whom the soul had was not the moral Law, but sin -- which by means of the Law is provocative of evil corruptions within the soul. When the believer is regenerated, then the soul is married to another, that is, to Christ. It is important also to observe that in working out the application of this analogy, the apostle does not say, the Law is dead, but that the believers have "become dead"; for, indeed, the Law is never so much alive as in the

godly who constantly obey it and live according to
it. Farther on in this passage Paul turns the thought
around and speaks of "that being dead wherein we
were held" (Romans vii. 6). The thing which is here
referred to as having died is interpreted by many
commentators as being sin. Sin having been put to
death -- by Christ -- the condemning and enslaving
power of the Law is at an end, and the believer becomes "married" to another.

There is nothing in the Scripture, therefore, to
give ground for the assumption that believers have
no obligation and relation to the Law of God. The
entire representation of the Christian life in the
epistles proves the contrary and calls for the believer's loving obedience to that holy Law.

CHAPTER XI

THE LAW AS A COVENANT

No clear conception of the place of the Law in the plan of salvation can be reached without understanding the significance of the Law in its covenant form. The Law was given this form when it was presented to the people at Mount Sinai: it bears the name of a covenant and possesses also the real properties of a covenant.

The name "covenant" is given to the Mosaic Law in a number of Scripture passages. Moses deals with those who commit wickedness as "transgressing his covenant" (Deuteronomy xvii. 2), words which the context shows to apply to the Ten Commandments. The Assyrian captivity of Samaria is said to be, "Because they obeyed not the voice of the Lord their God, but transgressed his covenant, and all that Moses the servant of the Lord commanded" (II Kings xviii. 12). The covenant nature of the Law is put even more expressly by Solomon at the dedication of the Temple when he says, "In it have I put the ark, wherein is the covenant of the Lord, that he made with the children of Israel".* Indeed, if terms are to be used exactly and strictly, the books of Moses and of the prophets cannot be so well called the Old Covenant as can the Law which was given on Mount Sinai.

The Law has the real properties of a covenant, namely, a mutual consent and stipulation on both sides. These are fully shown in the Biblical account of the giving of the Law at Mount Sinai (Exodus xxiv. 3-5). In this record the following things are

* II Chronicles vi. 11, and see Jeremiah xi. 2-4.

seen which belong to a covenant. Firstly, there is
God Himself expressing His consent and willingness
to be their God, if they will keep the commandments
which were there and then delivered to them;
secondly, there is the full consent of the people
and their ready willingness to obey the commandments; thirdly, because covenants used to be written
down for a memorial, Moses is seen writing the
terms in a book; and, fourthly, because covenants
used to be confirmed by visible signs, especially
by the killing of beasts and offering them in sacrifice, therefore this also is done, and half of the
blood is sprinkled on the people to show their voluntary covenanting. This covenant is renewed in
the plains of Moab, in the account of which it is
expressly said that the nation stood to enter into
covenant with God in order that He might establish them to be a people unto Himself and that He
might be a God to them.* From all this it is clear
that the Law was given as a Covenant.

The difficulties for the interpreter are not over
when it has been proved that the Law is a covenant,
for the greatest difficulty of all centres in deciding
what covenant it is. It has been observed already
that it is sometimes understood to be a Covenant of
Works, sometimes a mixed Covenant, and sometimes a subservient Covenant; but when all these
views have been examined it will be found best to
hold it to be a Covenant of Grace. But in what sense
is the Law a Covenant of Grace?

One explanation is that it was quite truly a Covenant of Grace, but that the Jews, by their corrupt
understanding, turned it into a Covenant of Works
and so made it contrary to Christ. On this view it
is accordingly held that when Paul argues against

* Deuteronomy xxix. 10-13, and see also Deuteronomy xxvi.
17,18.

the Law, as contrary to grace, he does so, not with respect to the Law as it truly is, but only as it was falsely regarded by the Jews, who made a contradiction where there was none. Another explanation makes the Law to be a Covenant of Grace, but very obscurely, and understands the Gospel and the Law to be the same in substance, but differing only as an acorn does from a full-grown oak tree. Yet another argument is that the Law may be considered either in a broad sense, as comprehending the whole doctrine and promise delivered on Mount Sinai, or it may be considered more narrowly as an abstract rule of righteousness which offers life upon no terms but perfect obedience. Taken in the former sense, the Law was a Covenant of Grace; but taken in the latter sense, as detached from the Mosaic administration of it, it was not of grace but of works.

That the Law, taken in the full context of its Mosaic administration, is a Covenant of Grace may be proved by many strong arguments.

Grace is seen, first of all, in the relation of the covenanting parties. Those entering into covenant are God on the one part and the Israelites on the other. God dealt with the Israelites at this time as their God and Father, and for this reason He regards Himself as one of their own. Paul speaks about the "Israelites, to whom pertaineth the adoption, and the glory, and the covenants, and the giving of the law, and the service of God, and the promises" (Romans ix. 4). Unless the Covenant alluded to were a Covenant of Grace, it could not possibly include terms like these.

Secondly, the blessings of the Covenant are easily recognised as blessings of grace, for among them is the pardon of sin; whereas in the Covenant of Works there is no room for either repentance or pardon. In the second command God is described as one showing mercy to thousands; but "law", strictly taken, does not accept those who humble themselves in contrition, rather does it curse every one who does not continue in all the things commanded. God proclaims Himself in this Covenant as gracious, and long-suffering, keeping mercy for thousands and forgiving iniquity (Exodus xxxiv. 6,7); and this He does on the occasion of the renewing of the two tablets of the Law; whereas, if the people of Israel had been strictly held to the Law, in its require-ment of perfect obedience and with no allowance for any failure, they must have perished without any hope at all.

Again, that the Law was a Covenant, not of works, but of grace, can be seen from the outward ratifi-cation of the Covenant. The visible seal which ratified the Covenant was that of sacrifice and sprinkling the people with blood. This ceremony pointed forward to Christ, because ultimate recon-ciliation could not possibly be made with a sinner through the mediation of any mortal man. The medi-ation of Moses is likewise to be understood typically, just as the sacrifices are to be understood typically. If this Covenant had been a Covenant of Works, how-ever, there would have been no mediator required, either typical or real. If Christ is thus the Mediator of the Law as a Covenant, the Antinomian distinction that makes the Sinaitic Law to be something "in the hand of Moses" in contrast to something "in the hand of Christ" cannot be upheld; for it is plain that on Mount Sinai the Law was in no other hand than the hand of Christ.

Finally, the grace of the Mosaic Covenant is to be seen in its identity with the Abrahamic. When God gives this Law to the Israelites He employs it as an argument of His love and grace to them, and so remembers what He has promised to Abra-ham. Through Moses He says to them, "Wherefore

it shall come to pass, if ye hearken to these judgments, and keep, and do them, that the Lord thy
God shall keep unto thee the covenant and the mercy
which he sware unto thy fathers" (Deuteronomy
vii. 12). But if the Law had been a Covenant of
Works, then God would have abrogated and broken
His covenant and promise of grace which He made
with Abraham and his seed. Therefore, when Paul
opposes the Law and the promise, making the in-
heritance to be by the latter and not by the former
(Galatians iii. 18), he must be understood to be
speaking of the Law in the strict sense of the word;
for it is plain that in the administration of this
Covenant of Law, Moses had regard to the promise
and made them identical.

It is not altogether unexpected that objections are
made to all this. These are made both from those
passages of Scripture where the Law and faith are
so directly opposed, and from those passages where
the Law is said to be a ministry of death and to work
wrath (Romans iv. 14; x. 3-8; Galatians iii. 18). But
in answer to these objections the following things
must be considered. The first is that if these passages were to be rigidly interpreted in this way,
then they would also imply that there was no grace,
or faith, or anything of Christ given to the people
of Israel; whereas it is recorded that they had the
adoption even though in a state of bondage. In the
second place, it must be remembered that as it is
said of the Law that it works death, so is it said of
the Gospel that it is the savour of death. Indeed,
men are said to have had no sin if Christ had not
come, and those who despised Christ are said to
receive severer judgment than those who despised
the Law of Moses. The working of death -- to keep
the apostle's phrase -- was, therefore, through
man's corruption: it did not belong essentially to

the Law. Again, it must not be forgotten that Paul speaks these seemingly derogatory words about the ceremonial Law also, yet all acknowledge that the ceremonial Law was an expression of grace. Lastly, it has again to be remarked that much of what these passages contain is true only in a relative sense, that is to say, according to the interpretation of the Jews, who taking the Law without Christ, made it a killing letter. The apostle's derogatory words must therefore be understood only of the Law as it is wrongly separated from Christ and put into opposition to His grace.

It will transform much thinking about the relation between Law and Gospel if it is thus rightly understood that the Law as a Covenant was an integral part of the inviolable Covenant of Grace which God made with His people through Abraham.

CHAPTER XII

THE OPPOSITION BETWEEN THE
LAW AND THE GOSPEL

Although the Law given by God to the Israelites was a Covenant of Grace, there is, nevertheless, a sense in which the Law and the Gospel may be said to oppose each other. This is clearly represented in the dialogue which Paul has with himself when he writes: "Where is boasting then? It is excluded. By what law? of works? Nay: but by the law of faith" (Romans iii. 27). Before the precise opposition between the Law and the Gospel can be shown, however, there are two fundamental principles -- already observed in passing -- which must be laid down as the basis of the discussion.

In the first place, the grounds of comparison must be equal. The Law and the Gospel can be compared with each other in two ways. On the one hand they may be compared solely in respect of the grace which God gave under the Old Covenant and under the New, and then they differ only in degree; for those under the Law truly enjoyed the grace and the Spirit of God. On the other hand the Law may be taken as consisting solely of commandments and be then compared with the Gospel in all its plenteous mercy and grace. This second method is, of course, an unequal comparison; for if the doctrine or letter of the Gospel be taken without the grace of God, that letter may be said to kill just as much as the letter of the Law.

In the second place, it is important in this inquiry to keep clearly in mind the different uses of the word "law"; for if the Law be taken in its purely commanding aspect and at the same time be understood as a Covenant of grace, there is a confusion of works and faith. If, however, "law" be taken in the wider and comprehensive sense, then no such opposition arises. It should also be observed that as the word "law" may be taken in these two ways, so also may the word "Gospel". The gospel can be taken largely, as when it signifies the whole doctrine that the apostles were to preach;* or else it can be taken more strictly, as in the angel's message, "Behold, I bring you good tidings" (Luke ii. 10). The contrast between Law and Gospel may accordingly be first shown in connection with the wider sense of the words and then in the more limited.

When Law and Gospel are expounded in the larger sense of the words, it is found that some comparisons are false and some are true. It is untrue, for example, to say that those who lived under the Law had nothing but temporal and earthly blessings.** This is based on the assumption that spiritual blessings were only promised in the Old Testament, but that they were not enjoyed by any till the New Testament. Hence it is argued that the Gospel began with Christ, and it is denied that the promise of Christ is ever called the Gospel. This is false, for although this promise is sometimes called the promise made to the fathers (Acts vii. 17; xiii. 32), yet it is at the same time also called the Gospel (Romans i. 2; x. 14,15). There are also clear passages of Scripture to confute this opinion, such as where Paul mentions Abraham and David as instances of justification and remission of sins (Romans iv. 1-12), and where he regards the Israelites as having enjoyed the same spiritual reality and

* For example, in Mark xvi. 15

** ut supra, p. 11

blessing in their sacraments as those of which the
Christian partakes (I Corinthians x).

The true differences between the Law and the
Gospel, taken in the larger sense, are four. The
first of these is that the difference between the Law
and the Gospel is accidental, not essential or sub-
stantial. This means that the division of the Covenant into the Old and New is not like the division
of the genus into its opposite species; but rather is
it a division of the subject, according to its several
accidental administrations. The Lutheran theologians oppose the Calvinists in this, and maintain
that the Covenant given by Moses was a Covenant
of Works, and so directly contrary to the Covenant
of grace. They acknowledge, indeed, that the fathers
were justified by Christ and had the same way of
salvation as Christian believers; but they make the
Covenant of Moses to be a Covenant of Works super-
added to the promise, presenting a condition of
perfect righteousness to the Israelites so that they
might be convinced of their folly in their self-
righteousness. But, as has been already proved,
the Mosaic Covenant was a Covenant of Grace; and
the right understanding of the words "law" and "gospel" easily resolves the problem which stumbled
the Lutherans at this point. There can be no doubt
that the spiritually-minded Israelite did not rest in
the sacrifices or sacraments themselves, but by
faith really experienced Christ in them, as does the
Christian.

The second difference between the Law and the
Gospel is in the degrees of their clearness in the
revelation of spiritual realities. The light in the Old
Covenant is compared to that of the night time; and
that in the New, to the light of the sun in a glorious
dawning day (II Peter i. 19). There is a difference
in the fulness with which these heavenly things are
presented in the respective Covenants, but no

difference in the things themselves. This difference of degree between the Law and the Gospel appears also in their measure of grace. It is with reference to this difference that the Scripture speaks as if those under the Old Testament had none at all, merely because there was not such a plentiful out- pouring of God's Spirit upon them. There were ex- ceptional persons, of course, such as Abraham and David, who experienced outstanding degrees of grace, but this was not according to the ordinary dispensation of God's grace at that time. The dif- ference in degree of spiritual revelation and grace between the Old Covenant and the New is compar- able to the manner in which -- to borrow and adapt an analogy from Paul -- "one star differeth from another in glory"; both are glorious, but one is greater than the other.

A third difference is that the condition of believers under the Law has the appearance of being more servile: their condition is likened to that of the sons of the bond-woman (Galatians iv. 30). Law was a more prominent feature in the first covenant, hence, Augustine makes **timor** and **amor** to be the difference between them. In the Law, God met sin- ful man with wrath; but in the Gospel, He meets man as the father did the returning prodigal son. This difference of condition is touched upon in the New Testament passage where the contrast is drawn between Mount Sinai and Mount Sion (Hebrews xii. 18-29). It is easy to make a mistake here, however, for the Israelites have to be considered in a twofold way: in one aspect of their relation to God they occupy the position of servants in a household, and in another they are looked upon as sons under age. This means, therefore, that they were not wholly excluded from the Spirit of adoption, for Paul is emphatic that the promises and adoption truly be- longed to them (Romans ix. 4).

A fourth difference between the Law and the Gospel is in their continuance. The Mosaic form of the Covenant of Grace was to endure only until Christ the fulness came: then as the scaffolding is pulled down when the house is built, so all those external ordinances were abolished when Christ Himself came. A torch is superfluous when the sun shines; a disciplinarian is not necessary to those who have obtained perfect maturity; milk is not suitable for those who live on solid meat. The chaff preserves the corn, but when the corn is gathered, the chaff is thrown away; when the fruit comes, the flower fades. It is therefore in this respect that the Law was to be outmoded and a better Covenant was to come in its place. The blessings of the Mosaic Covenant are called a "shadow" (Hebrews x. 1); and although a shadow shows the presence of a man, it does not live, or eat, or speak. In the same way, though the sacrifices shadowed Christ, they could not exhibit the real benefits that were to come by Him.

It remains now to consider the differences between the Law in the narrower sense, as requiring exact obedience and promising eternal life upon no other terms, and the Gospel similarly taken, as the simple proclamation of Christ and His saving mercy to a penitent sinner.

The first difference is that the Law, in some measure of it, is made known by natural light, and is therefore agreeable to a natural conscience. It has to be said "in some measure", for there is much of the duty of the Law that is now unknown to the natural conscience; nevertheless, the outward duties are certainly known, and accordingly, as the truth of them is discerned by natural light, so the will of man concurs in them as something that it is right to do. It is otherwise with the Gospel, however, for the very truth of it must be wholly revealed by God, and no natural insight in the world can ever discern or think out the wonderful remedy of justification and salvation by Christ. Further, as the Gospel is thus above knowledge so the heart is more averse to it. By this it is possible to see why it is such a hard thing for a sinner to believe, and why, even when loaded with guilt, he finds such difficulty in being persuaded to roll his burden upon Christ. The reason is that there is nothing in man's natural conscience to help him in this duty. Persuade a man against murder, theft, adultery, and natural conscience gives its support: but urge him to believe, and this is altogether above nature. Hence it is, also, that by nature men seek to be justified by the works they do, and justification by faith is repugnant to them.

The second difference is in their object. The Law demands a perfect righteousness and will admit of nothing less; but the Gospel comes to the sinner in his need and brings pardon through Christ. This, of course, is the main difference, and is a difference in which they can never be made one. Attempts have been made to obscure this great and important difference, marring the glory of the Gospel by re-introducing the doctrine of justification by works in another form, but Paul makes the direct contradiction that if it is of faith, then it is not of works. He does not distinguish between works of nature and works of grace, or between works of grace perfect and imperfect, but speaks absolutely, and thereby also excludes the rather subtle view which makes faith to justify as if it were a "work".

The third difference arises from the manner in which the blessings are obtained. Eternal life by the Law would have been obtained by way of debt and justice (Romans iv. 4). It must not be supposed, of course, that Adam in the state of innocence could have fully merited this at God's hands, or that God

strictly became man's debtor, seeing that Adam was
dependent on God for everything; but in some sense
it would have been true that eternal life would have
been by way of justice, and boasting would not have
been excluded. But in the Gospel all is of grace
through Christ; so that the broken and contrite heart
can never sufficiently admire the grace and goodness of God in it.

The fourth difference is in respect of the subject.
The Law, strictly taken, is only for those who have
a perfect and upright nature: therefore it is a Covenant of Friendship, without any necessity for a
mediator. There is, indeed, a good use to which it
can be put in urging it upon self-righteous men, to
bring them out of love with themselves; to hardened
sinners, that their hearts might be broken; and,
moreover, to the godly also, to teach them the fair
copy according to which they are to write; but in
respect of justification by it, none can have that
advantage save those who are perfectly holy. It is
different in the Gospel, for here it is the broken-
hearted sinner to whom the message is given.

Lastly, the Law differs from the Gospel in form.
The Law is conditional; but the Gospel absolute. The
question is sometimes raised whether the Gospel is
absolute or not, and whether it has duties or threatenings. The meaning of this question is not whether
the Gospel be so absolute that it does not require
faith as a condition, or whether it be so absolute that
it excludes all repentance and holiness; but whether
the Gospel promises eternal life to a man in recognition of any worth or disposition in the sinner, or
only to faith which apprehends Christ. The answer
is that if the Gospel be taken comprehensively, that
is to say, for the whole teaching of Christ and the
apostles, it cannot be denied that they urged the duty
of mortification and sanctification, even adding a
warning to those who neglected this duty; but if the

Gospel be taken in the simple sense of the proclamation of salvation, then it assures the guilty conscience of the forgiveness of sins through the blood
of Christ, without requiring any other duty as a condition.

All these contrasts and comparisons between the
Law and the Gospel, when rightly expounded, are
embraced comprehensively within the manifold
work of the Covenant of Grace to which both Law
and Gospel belong.

CHAPTER XIII

CHRIST AS THE END OF THE LAW

The authority for the title of this chapter is found in the words of Paul who says, "For Christ is the end of the law for righteousness to every one that believeth" (Romans x. 4). But what is the meaning of the word "end"? In the Scripture it has a twofold meaning. Sometimes it signifies the idea of conclusion or terminus;* and sometimes it is used for the idea of perfection and fulfilment.** In this latter sense the word may also include the idea of the end of intention, or the scope which the Law-giver had in mind when He gave the Law.

In the former of these meanings, Paul's words have been applied to the ceremonial Law, of which Christ truly is the termination and abolition (although He was also an end of perfection to it). Such an application is true in itself, but it is not strictly relevant to the argument of the apostle, who is here speaking of the kind of Law that was thought to produce righteousness, which Law, of course, is the moral Law. It is, therefore, to the moral Law that the apostle must be understood to refer, and, correspondingly, it is in the second of the meanings of the word "end" that Paul must be understood when he says that "Christ is the end of the law".

According as the Law is understood in its narrower or wider sense, so Christ may be said to be the end of the moral Law in two ways. Viewed more strictly, the Law requires perfect obedience and

* As in Mark xiii. 7: "the end is not yet"
** See I Timothy i. 5 and Romans xiii. 10.

condemns those who do not fulfil it. In this restricted sense Christ cannot be the intention of the
Law, for it is merely an accident of the Law that a
sinner crushed and condemned by it should seek
for a Saviour.*

The other way in which the Law may be viewed
is that larger one which sees it in its context of the
Covenant of Grace. In this respect it can be said
that Christ was intended directly and not by accident; that is to say, when God gave the Law to the
people of Israel, He intended that the discovery of
their inability to keep it should make them desire
and seek for Christ.

Aquinas has a good distinction about an end. He
says that an end is two-fold: it is either that to
which a thing naturally inclines of itself; or it is
that for which a thing is appointed and ordained
by the one who brings it into being. Now the end
of the Law to which naturally it inclines is eternal
life to be obtained by a perfect righteousness in
man; but the instituted and appointed end, which
God the Law-giver made in the promulgation of it,
was for the purpose of provoking the Israelites to
seek Christ. They were not to rest in those commandments or duties, but to go on to Christ; so that
a believer was not to rejoice in any thing in the Law
till he came to Christ, and when he had found Him,
he was to seek no farther but to abide there.

When the Law is taken in its wider sense, it is
easy to see that Christ is the fulfilment of its

---

* It should not be forgotten that the Law does not exclude a
Saviour, even when it is taken in this strict way. It certainly
requires perfect righteousness, yet if a sinner brings the righteousness of a surety, though this be not commanded by the Law,
yet it is not against the Law or excluded by it; otherwise it would
have been injustice in God to have accepted Christ the Surety for
sinners.

appointed end. But it now remains to ask what this appointed end is.

First of all, it is the Divine intention in the Law to lead sinners to Christ. It was one of the weaknesses of the Israelites, that they were unable to look steadfastly to the end of that ministry of Moses, which end, of course, was Christ (II Corinthians iii. 7-16). Christ was thus the glorious Object in the administration of the Law, but the vail upon the Israelites' heart hindered the sight of it. Another instance which proves that Christ was the end of intention in the giving of the Law is found in the words, "We were kept under the law, shut up unto the faith which should afterwards be revealed. Wherefore the law was our schoolmaster to bring us unto Christ" (Galatians iii. 23,24). In these words, not the moral Law simply taken, but the whole Mosaic Covenant is compared to the guidance and discipline of a schoolmaster. The Law did not only curb man's sin, but also revealed Christ; it did not merely threaten and curse, but showed that help was to be found in Christ alone.

Secondly, it is the Divine intention in the Law to accept those who fulfil it. By reason of the fall it is impossible for man to attain this end, but Christ has brought about this intent of the Law in the justification and eternal life of those who trust in Him. If the end of human laws is to make good and honest men, much more so is this the end of the moral Law appointed by God Himself; but so far is the Law from making a man good that it produces all kinds of evil in him, an effect of the Law which Paul acknowledges to have taken place in himself. Just as food received by a diseased body does nothing but increase the disease, so also it comes to pass that the Law, which is designed to produce goodness and life, becomes the cause of sin and death. In order that the Law may have its true end, therefore, Christ takes human nature upon Him so that the righteousness of the Law might be fulfilled in those whom He redeems.

Thirdly, it is the Divine intention in the Law to justify the sinner through the merits of Christ. This is realised as Christ's obedience to the Law is reckoned to the believer, and so in Him as a Surety the Law is fulfilled. This truth is contradicted by many, but it is supported by the parallel which Paul draws between the first Adam and his seed, on the one hand, and Christ, the second Adam, and His seed, on the other. In this parallelism the apostle proves that believers are made righteous by the imputation of the righteousness of Christ (Romans v. 12-21). The same argument is again employed by Paul when he teaches that as Christ was "made sin" by imputation, so are believers given the righteousness of God in Him (II Corinthians v. 19,20). Similarly, when he says that God sent His Son that the righteousness of the Law might be fulfilled in those who walk not after the flesh but after the Spirit (Romans viii. 3,4), he is implying the same truth. The objection is sometimes raised that if the righteousness of Christ be made man's, so that he may be said to fulfil the Law, then he is still justified by a Covenant of Works and there is no new Covenant of Grace. The answer to this is that, because of Christ's fulfilment of the Law as Surety for the sinner, a man truly obtains eternal life according to the rule "do this and live"; for the imputation of righteousness does not make it cease to be real righteousness, even though it be not a man's own inherent righteousness. There is no reason at all, however, to infer from this that eternal life is legally bestowed on the basis of a Covenant of Works, for this righteousness comes to the sinner not by working but by believing.

In one of His discussions with the Jews about
Moses, Christ said, "he wrote of me", and there is
no true appreciation of the work of Moses if Christ
is not thus seen to be the "end" of all his ministry.

CHAPTER XIV

EPILOGUE

Little needs to be said in conclusion, save to stress the obvious and sacred importance which God in the Scripture attaches to the observance of His holy Law. This must be taken to heart by the believer and the preacher alike. The believer must increasingly delight in it "after the inward man" (Romans vii. 22), demonstrating the truth of the Lord's saying, "If a man love me, he will keep my words" (John xiv. 24). The preacher, likewise, must seek the help of the Holy Spirit so to preach the Gospel that he honours the Law, and so to expound the Law that he sends men to the Gospel. It brings no praise to God when either of these glorious manifestations of His ways is neglected.

Let almost the last word be with one of the later Puritans from Scotland. As a means of aiding the memory of their hearers, the preachers of the 17th and 18th centuries occasionally produced a versification of their sermons. These versifications could scarcely be called poetry, but their rhythm and rhyme greatly assisted in the retention of the truths contained in them. Ralph Erskine produced a rhyme of this sort in which he indicated the Puritan views on the place of Law in the believer's life. Here is part of a sonnet of 386 verses which he entitles "The Believer's Principles concerning the Law and the Gospel." Section III is called "The Harmony betwixt the Law and the Gospel."

. . . .

The law's a tutor much in vogue,
To gospel-grace a pedagogue;
The gospel to the law no less
Than its full end for righteousness.

When once the fiery law of God
Has chas'd me to the gospel-road;
Then back unto the holy law
Most kindly gospel-grace will draw.

When by the law to grace I'm school'd;
Grace by the law will have me rul'd;
Hence, if I don't the law obey,
I cannot keep the gospel-way.

When I the gospel-news believe,
Obedience to the law I give:
And that both in its fed'ral dress,
And as a rule of holiness.

. . . .

What in the gospel-mint is coin'd,
The same is in the law injoin'd:
Whatever gospel-tidings teach,
The law's authority doth reach.

Here join the law and gospel hands,
What this me teaches that commands:
What virtuous forms the gospel please
The same the law doth authorise.

And thus the law-commandment seals
Whatever gospel-grace reveals:
The gospel also for my good
Seals all the law-demands with blood.

The law most perfect still remains,
And ev'ry duty full contains:
The Gospel its perfection speaks,
And therefore gives whate'er it seeks.

. . . .

Law-threats and precepts both, I see,
With gospel-promises agree;
They to the gospel are a fence,
And it to them a maintenance.

The law will justify all those
Who with the gospel-ransom close;
The gospel too approves for ay
All those that do the law obey.

. . . .

A rigid master was the law,
Demanding brick, denying straw;
But when with gospel-tongue it sings,
It bids me fly, and gives me wings.

In this paradox lies the perfect wisdom of God, and the appropriate prayer of the true believer may well be that of the psalmist, "Give me understanding, and I shall keep thy law; yea, I shall observe it with my whole heart" (Psalm cxix. 34).

APPENDICES

APPENDICES

I. HISTORICAL NOTE
Anthony Burgess

Anthony Burgess, the substance of whose work on the Law of God is taken up into this volume, is honoured with a place in the Dictionary of National Biography and is also included in Palmer and Calamy's account of the lives and printed works of the two thousand ministers who were ejected from the Church of England in 1662. The dates of his birth and death do not seem to be known, but the period of his literary activities extended from the year 1646 until about 1659. The son of a schoolmaster at Watford, Hertfordshire, he entered St. John's College, Cambridge, in 1623 and graduated as Master of Arts. Subsequently, he became a Fellow of Emmanual College. For a number of years he was Vicar of Sutton Coldfield, Warwickshire, but after the restoration of the monarchy he was ejected from Sutton Coldfield and went to reside at Tamworth. He was a respected member of the Westminster Assembly. Of his written works, **Vindiciae Legis: or, A Vindication of the Morall Law and the Covenants,** was his first, being produced in 1646, and it was followed by **The True Doctrine of Justification** (1648), **A Treatise of Grace and Assurance** (1652), **A Treatise of Sinne** (1654), **Sermons on the Seventeenth of John** (1656), **The Scripture Directory,** and the **Doctrine of Original Sin** (1659).

Like many other Puritan writings, **Vindiciae Legis** consists of the material preached by the author in the course of his regular pulpit ministry. It was first published as a series of twenty-nine lectures, but in the following year the second edition appeared and contained thirty lectures. The work was dedicated by the author "To the truly pious and worthily honoured Lady, the Lady RUTH SCUDAMORE". In the dedication, dated 21st. September, 1646, he writes,

"Honoured Madam,

I have observed your Ladyship careful in two things: to improve the duty commanded in the Law, and to embrace the promise tendered in the Gospel; the former hath been a spur to holiness, the latter a curb to unbelief.

...God hath left your mind fixed and immovable in the truth, being enabled to magnify Grace in the highest manner, out of the real sense of your necessity and unworthiness, yet to avoid Antinomianism: and on the other side, to be punctual and exact in the duties of mortification and holiness; yet to take heed to Pharisaical Popery. And indeed, this is the right sense, when we are so diligent in working out our salvation with fear and trembling, as if there were no grace to justify; and yet so resting and believing in the grace of Christ, as if no good thing had been done by us..."

Both the editions carried with them the following prefaced commendation:

"We the President and Fellows of Sion College London, earnestly desire Master Anthony Burgess to publish in print his elaborate and judicious Lectures upon the Law and the Covenants

against the Antinomian errors of these times,
which at our entreaty he hath preached, (and
for which we give him most hearty thanks) that
so well the Kingdom as this City, may have the
benefit of those his learned labours.

ARTHUR JACKSON President, in
the name and by the appointment of the rest.
Dated at Sion College, the 11th. June 1646, at a
general meeting of the Ministers of London
there."

The title page of the second edition of the work
reads as follows:

VINDICIAE LEGIS: or, A Vindication of the
Morall Law and the Covenants, From the Er-
rours of Papists, Arminians, Socinians, and
more especially Antinomians. In XXX LEC-
TURES, preached at Laurence-Jury, London.
The second Edition corrected and augmented.
By Anthony Burgess, Preacher of God's Word.
LONDON, Printed by James Young, for Thomas
Underhill, at the Signe of the Bible in Wood-
street, 1647.

Anthony Burgess reveals himself as a scholarly,
cultured and well-read man; indeed, the Bishop of
Lichfield regarded him as equal in learning to a
university professor. His work contains many
Greek and Latin quotations; he shows himself familiar with the writings of Aristotle, Seneca, Augustine, Aquinas, Luther and Calvin. He does not
merely display literary ability, however, for he has
the homely devotional language of the experimental
preacher combined with a gift of penetrative ideas.
Here are one or two sentences that stand out in

these ways. "He that distinguisheth well, teacheth well"; "It is not every man that talketh of grace doth therefore set up Scripture-grace"; "How uncomfortable will it be when thou diest, to commit thy soul to that grace which thou hast disputed against"; "Take the Law for a goad, the Gospel for a cordial: from the one be instructed, from the other supported... The Law hath a loveliness in it as well as the Gospel"; "How necessary a duty it is for a Minister of Jesus Christ to be diligent in preaching and explicating of the Law of God... The preaching of the Law is so necessary, that you can never be spiritual, heavenly, heart-Christians, unless these things be daily set before your eyes... Oh know, there is a great deal of unknown sinfulness in thy heart, because the Law is unknown to thee".

The book consists of two hundred and eighty one closely-printed pages. There is a Table of Contents extending to six pages and a Textual Index of one full page. As was the style of the time, the text is divided into numbered paragraphs with italicised headings to show the pattern of the argument as it proceeds. The Puritans employed their logic in a forceful and captivating manner, and Anthony Burgess is no exception to this, for he allows no proposition to stand without subjecting it to searching analysis. A sympathetic appreciation of his thorough-going methods of logical analysis, however, will greatly assist in grasping both the richness and the sustained strength of his argument. There is a deeply-ordered precision in Anthony Burgess's reasoning, and the multitude of meticulous definitions, which sometimes look like disorder, contribute to the profound coherence and unity of his closely-knit argument.

The object of the book is stated by the author in his address, "To the Reader". "For the matter of it", he says, "it is chiefly improved to maintain the dignity and use of the Moral Law against late errors

dignity and use of the Moral Law against late errors about it . . ." His immediate concern is not so much with justification as with sanctification and the place which the moral Law must have as a rule of life to believers. Is it true that the justified believer has "finished with Moses"? This question, he says, is put too simply, for no useful answer can be given until it is made clear in what sense the question is to be understood. If it is concerned with justification and the ground of a sinner's acceptance with God, then, of course, the justified believer is most certainly "finished with Moses" (though it has to be interjected here that "Moses" was never intended for such a purpose). If, however, the question is concerned with the behaviour of the believer and what things are pleasing or displeasing to God, then, equally emphatically, the answer must be returned that the justified believer is not "finished with Moses".

But Anthony Burgess contends that the subject may not be dismissed so easily as this, and he asks, What authority is there for putting Moses and Christ into opposite camps? What ground is there for the assumption that the Law of God is contrary to the Grace of God? When he examines these questions he shows that no antagonism or contrariety exists between Law and Grace. Moses is the minister of Christ, and "the Law is ancient grace". It is, therefore, no departure from the principle of grace that a believer keeps the Law of God and hallows it in its true nature as "law".

Copies of **Vindiciae Legis** are extremely rare.

II. SUBJECT INDEX

III. TEXTUAL INDEX

Job

Psalms

Isaiah

Jeremiah

Hosea

Micah

Matthew

Mark

Luke

John

John (continued)

Acts

Romans

Romans (continued)

AN EXPOSITION OF
THE TENTH COMMANDMENT
by
LANCELOT ANDREWES

"Thou shalt not covet Thy neighbor's house. Thou shalt not covet thy neighbor's wife."—Exodus 20:17

The dependence of this commandment upon the rest appears in this, that without the observing of this none of the rest can be kept. For by giving this after all the rest, God would teach us how all the rest are to be understood, viz. that not only the outward act is forbidden in them, but also the inward purpose and intention of the heart (even if we never proceed to the outward act). So that this is the rule and the measure for the understanding and for observing the rest of the commandments—this is the hinge upon which all the rest turn. Therefore St. Augustine says that he who would observe the rest must chiefly look to the keeping of this commandment, for this one looks to the heart. And out of the heart, as Solomon says, "proceed the issues of life" and death, and therefore he advises us "to keep the heart with all diligence." (Prov. 4:23).

The scope and end of the Lawgiver in this is twofold:

1. To show that He looks further than His substitutes on earth can do, and that His Law has a pre-eminence above theirs. For though man's law may bind the hands and the feet, it may put a stop to the mouth and may condemn the purpose of the heart (so far as it can take hold or discover—for if one be found with a weapon, or breaking into a house, though he be kept back from the act of murder or robbery, yet here his purpose is discovered and taken hold of, and therefore he is punished by man's law,) but all human laws—and it is and axiom in the Civil Law—say let no man suffer for bare thoughts. And so they let thoughts go free. But God takes order for the very thoughts, though they do not appear by any overt act. And therefore Simon Magus is brought to the bar for the thought of his heart, "Pray," saith he, "if perhaps the thought of your heart may be forgiven you." (Acts 8:22).

2. It is for those who, Pharisee-like, are conceited as to their own righteousness, so that these proud sinners who are not healed may by this Law be convicted of their need of a Physician. For though a man in regard to the full consent of heart hold out and justify himself in some things, and for some small time, yet when he comes to this commandment in which the imperfect birth (when there is not a perfect consent, only some pleasure and titillation in the motion of the heart) is forbidden, this will make him sweat. It will make him cry out, "O wretched man that I am, who shall

137

deliver me from the body of death," (Romans 7:25), and so it will make him see that he cannot acquit himself nor be a Christ or Saviour to himself. But he knows that he must flee to another outside of himself, as it is in the next words, "I thank God through the Lord Jesus Christ, etc."

For the consent of the heart is forbidden by the other commandments, as they are expounded by our Saviour, who says that "if a man looks upon a woman (with this purpose and mind) to lust after her," then this is adultery. But here the intention and desire, even though it does not have full consent, being only an imperfect one, is tainted by this precept.

Here is the distinction: In the former commandments the intention of evil is forbidden, though it is not executed, and here also, even though it is not prosecuted or resolved upon (as when the motion is entertained with approval or delight, though not fully consented to). St. Augustine explains the matter in this way: In the one case you have a "Thou shalt not lust," forbidden by this commandment; and in the other case a "follow not after your lusts," (Ecclus. 18:30), and he that has attained the latter, says the same father, has done much but he has not done all, because he still is lusting.

The Apostle Paul distinguishes between them in this way: he calls the one "sin reigning in us," when "we follow it in the lusts of it;" and the other he calls "sin dwelling in us," when it lusts in us but has not gotten a perfect dominion. In this latter case it dwells as a private person, but in the former it rules, it has the kingdom. For when sin has so far prevailed both upon our affections and upon our reason that there lacks only an opportunity to act it, then it reigns. But when we have given some entertainment to it in our minds, so that there is a reasoning within us (a "shall I do it, or shall I not?") when we have reasons pro and con and are not fully resolved, then sin dwells in us and this is properly forbidden by this commandment. If we once resolve fully, "I will do it!" then it is as good as done before God, and then it may be referred to the other commandments as forbidden there also.

THE THING PROHIBITED, CONCUPISCENCE, OR LUST

It either (1) arises from ourselves, or (2) from the Spirit of God. When from ourselves, it is either (1) from nature, or (2) from the corruption of nature. Corrupt desires are of two sorts, either (1) vain and foolish, or (2) hurtful or injurious.

1. There is a concupiscence of our own, of which St. Peter speaks "There shall come men walking after their own lusts."

2. There is a lust of the spirit, of which the Apostle says that "it lusts against the flesh." This is holy and good, for when our

minds are enlightened by the Spirit of God, it stirs up in us good motions and desires. It strengthens us to bring the same into effect, and it arms us against the opposition with which we meet. By this lust, evil motions are checked when they arise in the heart. We see this in the Psalmist, "Why art thou cast down O my soul, and why art thou disquieted within me? Trust in the Lord, etc." This lust, then, is not condemned here, but as it is in itself acceptable, so "by helping our infirmities," it makes our prayers acceptable with God. And by procuring audience with Him, by which we obtain our desires of God, it increases in us love to God and to men. This therefore is not restrained by this tenth commandment, but the other lust, which is properly called lust, is our own lust.

THIS LUST OF OUR OWN IS OF TWO SORTS

The first is natural, the second is from the corruption of nature, which St. Peter calls "the lust of corruption," or "corrupt lust." The first, natural lust, is in men by nature, as to lust for meat when one is hundry, or to drink when he is thirsty. And this is not forbidden, for it was in Christ Himself, who was free from all sin. He was sometimes hungry and desired food, and He was sometimes weary and desired rest, etc. But in the other, the corrupt lusts or desires which are forbidden in this place. This faculty of desiring or lusting was at first given to the soul to make it move toward those objects which the mind propounds. As there is lightness in some things to make them move upwards, so the heathen called the mind the eye of the soul. And they called the desire or the appetite the motion or endeavor of the soul after that which the eye discerns. But this desire or lust being corrupt chokes the light of the mind, so that it cannot direct to what is good. For the faculties of the soul, being joined together, corrupt and infect one another—as ivy that cleaves to the oak and draws away the sap and makes it wither. And so the mind being blinded, the will cannot move towards that which is good, and so our desires become corrupt.

OUT OF THIS CORRUPT LUST SPRINGS DESIRES OF TWO SORTS

They are distinguished by St. Paul, some are vain and foolish—others are hurtful and injurious.

The first we see in such men as the Apostle called "earthly minded," who desire worldly things, not for natural ends only, passing and leaping over the bounds of nature, desiring more than is necessary. For they still desire more and more, and as the Psalmist speaks, "when their riches increase, they set their hearts upon them," which the words before imply is foolishness and vanity. Such men think, speak and delight to talk of nothing but earthly things, and so they at length corrupt themselves. As the Prophet speaks, "their silver has become dross and their wine mixed with water," when they mingle their souls with earthly things which are of an inferior and baser condition than the soul.

The other desires which he calls "hurtful" are those properly which are opposed by the Spirit of God (Galatians 5). And these lusts keep us back from good things, which the Spirit suggests, because there is a foreskin which has grown over the heart, which shuts up and closes the heart when any good motion is offered. And this foreskin of the heart leaves it open when any evil would enter. There is also a foreskin drawn over the ears ("O ye of uncircumcised hearts and ears," (Acts 7:51) by which the like effects are worked, for it shuts the ears against anything that is good and draws the covering aside for corrupt or unsavory communication to enter in. Because of this, God is said "to uncover the ear" when He reforms men effectually. (See Job 33:16)

And secondly, as they keep us back from receiving good, so they corrupt that good which is already in us, like the dead fly in the box of ointment (Eccles. 10:1).

And thirdly, they provoke us to evil, or, which is all one, to such things as are not in themselves evil but which will ensnare us in evil if we follow them. For evil, whether in the antecedents or in the consequents of it, is evil, and it is to be avoided. Therefore the Apostle would not have us to be "brought under the power of anything," because the Devil sometimes kindles such an earnest desire in a man after some lawful indifferent thing, so that he will not forego it for any reason. Then the Devil will quickly find a condition to annex to it, by which he will draw a man to something simply unlawful. This he thought he could do with Christ when he showed Him the kingdoms of the world and the glory of them, with which he thought he had wrought upon His affections, seeking presently to draw Him to idolatry, "All these I will give Thee if Thou wilt fall down and worship me."

So the desires of our concupiscence are evil. As St. Augustine says, either we desire to get things lawful by evil means, or, if we try by lawful means, yet it is for an evil end. And both these ways of getting are justly condemned, even in the very desire of the heart.

This concupiscence and these strong desires proceeding from it are expressed in Scripture by other words. Sometimes it is called "the old man," sometimes "sin dwelling in us," sometimes "the law of sin," and the "law of the members." Sometimes it is the "sting of death," sometimes "the prick in the flesh," sometimes "the sin which so easily besets us," sometimes "fleshly lusts which war against the soul," sometimes "the poison of the serpent," which the Devil instilled into our nature at the first. The Schoolmen call it the "inbred fuel of sin." Others call it the disorder or irregularity of the faculties of the soul, because man had advanced his lust above his reason, against the order and will of God, and so made it chief, and in order to fulfil his desire he hazarded the favor of God. Therefore, as a just punishment, God has so ordered in His wrath that it should be stronger than reason, so that it cannot be brought under that superior faculty, even if a man desires it. So that as God said by the prophet (and a fearful judgment it is!) "because Ephraim had made altars to sin, therefore they should be sin to him." So here, because man would have his lust to be superior, it shall indeed be superior, do what he can. So God in great wrath sometimes deals with men, as He did with the Israelites, "they ate and were filled to the full, and He gave them their own desire, they were not disappointed of their lust." (Psalm 78:29,30) In another place, "He gave them up to their own heart's lusts and to follow their own imaginations. So he dealt with the heathen Romans after great disobedience and willful sinning against the light of their own hearts, there follows this (Romans 1:28), "God gave them up to their own desires, counsels, inventions and imaginations."

This is a fearful thing, to be given up to a man's own lust. It is much to be delivered over to Satan. Yet he who has been turned over to Satan has a return, for he that was so given up was regained (1 Cor. 5:7, 2 Cor. 2:7). But when a man is delivered up to himself, it is certain, at least by ordinary means, that he never returns again. For this is that "reprobate mind" which the Apostle mentions, when God gives a man completely over, withdrawing His grace and leaving him in his own hands to final destruction. So that it is better to be delivered over to the Devil than to his own will. And so we see how well we are to think of our own will, and we see how dreadful a thing it is to be given over to it, not having God's Spirit to maintain a perpetual conflict with our own corrupt lusts.

HOW A MAN COMES TO BE GIVEN UP TO HIS OWN DESIRES

Now for the means by which a man comes to be thus endangered, it has been partly revealed in the first commandment, where our duty to God answers to our duty towards our neighbor in this commandment. A man comes to be given up to his own desires by degrees, when he gives way to evil imaginations against his neighbor. "Let no man imagine or think evil in his heart against his neighbor" (Zech. 8:17). We must not give way to it at all, we must not allow it to fester. There is in every one of us an evil imagination against our neighbor, to do them prejudice. And this being in us, then there comes in a temptation, as the Apostle shows us in Ephes. 2:2,3, partly from the world ("according to the course of the world,") partly from the Devil, who then begins to strike and to work and fashion the thought of the heart toward a perfect sin ("according to the prince of the power of the air,"). So they both work upon our thoughts and desires "to fulfil the lusts of the flesh."

So there is a double cause to draw us to this: 1, our lust alone, considered in itself, as it rises by itself, without any blowing or quickening of it from without, and 2, as it is employed and wrought by the world, or the Devil, or by both.

1. By itself alone. Christ speaks of "evil thoughts that proceed out of the heart," and "of thoughts that arise in the heart." (Matt. 15 and Mark 7). There is a steam or vapor which arises from our nature, for evil thoughts rise up or ascend from below, and good thoughts come or descend from above (James 1:18). The one comes from ourselves, the other from God and His Spirit. Now the Devil knows this and takes occasion by those desires which he sees by some outward sign to arise within us, assaulting us by propounding worldly objects and allurements, making use of the world to tempt us. So he dealt with Christ, leaving Him alone until He was hungry and had His "natural desire for bread." Then he comes to Him and offers Him "stones to be turned into bread," thinking by that means (when Christ had a natural appetite) to have been received.

2. As there are thoughts ascending into the heart, so there are another sort of thoughts, those cast in by the Devil. So the Devil entered into Judas when he put those evil thoughts into his heart of betraying his Master. And so he filled the heart of Ananias and Sapphira to lie to the Holy Spirit and to commit sacrilege. And as he sometimes does this immediately from himself, so he also sometimes makes use of the world and of outward objects to cast evil thoughts into our hearts. So the world and the Devil infect us from without, when we are also reinfecting ourselves fast enough from within. For as Nazianzen speaks, the spark is within us, the flame is from the evil spirit blowing it up. So that even though there were no devil to tempt us, even though we were in the wilderness where no worldly objects could lure us, yet we carry enough in our bosoms to corrupt ourselves. Neither can we be safe though we leave all the world behind us, so long as we carry our own hearts with us, says Basil.

EVIL THOUGHTS COMING FROM WITHIN US ARE SIN, THOSE COMING FROM WITHOUT US ARE NOT.

The ascending thoughts within us are sin, but those that are sent into us, those that are injected into us, (unless we give way to them, allowing them to infect us,) are our crosses, not our sins. Nay, by resisting these motions and temptations of Satan, we win the crown, and every temptation we resist is a new flower in our garland.

How do these thoughts come to infect us? There are six degrees before we come to that full consent and purpose of heart which is forbidden by the other commandments. In Genesis, when Eve was tempted, we see how the infection began. There is the fruit held out, the object to allure, and with it the three provocations by which all sins are ushered into the soul are there set down.

1. It was good to eat—the lure of profit.

2. It was pleasing and delightful to the eye—here is the bait of pleasure.

3. It is said to be desired in regard to knowledge—here is the appeal to pride. These three are mentioned by St. John, "the lust of the flesh, the lust of the eye, and the pride of life." (1 John 2:16)

4. And in the next verse, the Devil adds a fourth (which may be reduced to the third,) "You shall be as gods." The very lure of pride is excellency, a condition to be desired by man, being chief of the creatures. These being held out, every one was paused upon by Eve, she had respective regard to all of them, "for the woman seeing that the tree was good for food and pleasing to the eyes, and a tree to be desired to make one wise, she took of the fruit of it, and ate." Out of which we may observe these several steps and degrees by which sin enters into the soul:

1. The first is called "a turning back after Satan," (1 Tim. 5:15) or a turning of the soul back to look on the object. The first entertaining of it is a turning of the soul from God, which when one does it, he begins to prostitute his soul to the Devil.

2. The second is when the object suits them perfectly, that they eagerly desire it. This may be sudden, a light motion upon the first sight. Or it may be more earnestly impressed upon us, a more earnest or violent passion. Job compares him that has gone this far to one "that has a sweet poison in his mouth," who because of the sweetness that he feels is reluctant to spit it out—he will not let it go, nor yet does he dare swallow it, but he keeps it under his tongue. Thus a light motion becomes a violent passion, and this is a keeping and retaining of the seed, as the first light motion was a receiving of the seed. And as in that there was a turning from God, so in this there is a turning to the creature.

3. The third is a consent to take delight in it. For as before there was a double consent, (1) a consent to execute or act the sin (this may be forbidden in the other commandments and is that which we called the inward festering of our hereditary wound; and (2) a consent in mind only to take pleasure in it, by often spurring of the heart toward it—in which we so far consent to it as to delight in the thought of it, though as yet we have no full purpose to act it, thinking only to gaze and stare at it—this they call the conceiving of sin (James 1:15).

4. The fourth is a delaying or lingering in the thought of it, so that when a man has once consented to go so far as to take pleasure in it, he will stay by it and dwell in it. This is the framing of all the parts in the womb of the soul, by which it becomes complete, when every corner is searched and every circumstance is weighed and considered, as to how the sin is to be acted. When the people remained at Shittim, the people committed fornication with the daughters of Moab! (Numbers 25:1).

5. There is then the wandering of the soul after it. That is, when the thoughts have passed over it, yet we recall them and make a covenant contrary to that of Job's, that we will not allow our eyes to look away from the alluring object. But we must still behold it, and not only so, but we also employ those gates and passages to the fancy, the senses, to raise up this delight in us again, that we may continue in it. We read in Genesis of the imagination of the thoughts of the heart (Gen. 6:5), when there is no real object, and yet a man will nevertheless frame or imagine a false object to convince the pleasure of a thought. So here is a framing of imaginations to please the soul in such a sinful thought, when besides occasions offered, a man procures to himself occasions outwardly, or inwardly devises fancies to delight himself. This is the quickening of sin when it begins to stir in the womb.

6. The last is the travail, or birth. It is a laying hold on the occasion offered in order to act the sin formerly resolved upon. It proceeds on a syllogism like this : If there is so much pleasure in thinking of it and revolving it in my mind, then what pleasure must there be when it is actually performed? After this comes the full consent of the mind, and then we are out of this commandment, for there is nothing lacking but the means and opportunity to act it. The conclusion is set down in the heart, I will do it! Then, when the occasion is offered, it is done. And so sin is brought forth and perfected.

And these are the six degrees of sin, although sin flatters and lies to itself, persuading men that they are not guilty until they come to the last degree, the very act—but there is sin in all the rest.

THE WAYS BY WHICH A MAN IS TEMPTED BY HIS OWN LUST

First, there is a bait, then there is a hook. St. James mentions two ways by which a man is tempted by his lust: (1) he is either drawn by a kind of violence, or (2), he is enticed by some allurement, "Every man is tempted when he is drawn away by his own lust, and enticed." (James 1:14). There is a pretty enticing bait to allure, and there is a violent, pushing and haling of the soul by force. For a man is drawn either by the pleasure of the sense, or else by the importunity of the mind. Either sin gets within us and lures us on until we are caught, or else it assaults us in a boistrous manner so that we yield and think that we can do nothing else. Against both of these we must watch, lest we be like those in Hosea, "They have made their heart ready like an oven, the Baker sleeps all night, in the morning it burns like a flaming fire. They are all hot as an oven,—there is none that calls upon Me." (Hosea 7:5).

The other two, the World and the Devil, tempt us in the same order. There is the alluring and the drawing in both of them.

The Devil is called "the old serpent" in Scripture, and the Apostle speaks of his "method of craftiness," and his "deceit," by which men are deceived (Eph. 6). We know that the serpent is subtle by nature, but he is an old serpent, who, if he had any natural defect, might by custom and long experience have supplied it. Again, the Apostle speaks of the tricks and wiles of the Devil. The apostles were not ignorant of them, but another may fear lest it be the Devil's method and craft by which he is lured away. And he should fear lest he be not wise enough of himself to discern it.

2. He is called a "roaring lion." And under these two names, a serpent and a lion, all that is spoken of him in Scripture may be included. As he is a serpent for his subtlety, so for his strength, violence and cruelty he is called a lion, and a roaring lion. When he had permission given him, we see that he made the swine run headlong into the sea, with violence. And the Apostle tells us that he torments with "fightings without and terrors within," (2 Cor. 7:5). And though the Apostle had a good purpose in coming to the Thessalonians, to have confirmed their faith, yet "Satan hindered him." The Apostles had extraordinary knowledge to discern his tricks, and power to oppose his violence, which we do not have. Therefore we must stand upon our watch the more diligently, and we must put on our spiritual armor so that we may be able to oppose him. This extreme violence and exceeding subtlety in persuasion will betray whether the temptation comes from within ourselves, or if it comes from the Devil on the outside.

And as we say of him, so we may say of the World. It tempts sometimes by attractive means, using subtlety, offering pleasures and profits, preferments, etc. to lure us. And if we will not be lured, there is a hook to draw us. Instead of profit (it will tell us) you shall have damage and loss—instead of pleasure, grief—and instead of preferment, reproach and disgrace shall come—all that it may prevail against us and bear us down. St. Augustine says that either the love of the bait will inflame us, or the fear of the hook will frighten us, to draw us on to evil, or to keep us back from good. So we see that all temptations to evil may be reduced to these three heads: They come either from "the world, the flesh, or the Devil." All of these seek to lure us, either by the bait, or by the hook.

We see then the negative part of this commandment, in the words expressed. Now because according to rule, the affirmative is implied in the negative, we shall say something of the affirmative part.

THE AFFIRMATIVE PART OF THE COMMANDMENT

This is set down by the Apostle when he exhorts us, "to be renewed in the spirit of your minds," and "to put on the new man which is renewed in knowledge after the image of Him that created him," and "to become new creatures." (Eph. 4:23, Col. 3:10, Gal. 6.15). We must labor, he prayed, that "our spirit, soul and body may be sanctified and preserved blameless unto the coming of Christ." (1 Thess. 5:23). We must "mortify our earthly members," our carnal lusts and affections, and "crucify the old man," so that sin may not reign in our mortal bodies (Col. 3:5). Not only must the mind be renewed, but the will also must be renewed, it must be brought into subjection to the will of God, so that we may be able to say with David, "Here am I, let God do with me as He pleases," and with Christ, "Not My will, but Thy will be done." Our inward man is corrupt in all the faculties, the understanding is darkened and the will is perverted. For as in old men there is a dimness of sight and weakness in the members, so in this old man which we are to put off there is blindness of mind and weakness of spirit, and they must be renewed.

Though sin be in itself a transient act, yet after the act there is something that remains and this is that which requires a renewal. There is (1) the guilt, which makes us unworthy of favor and worthy of punishment. And (2) there is the stain, which renders us filthy and deformed. Then (3) there is the wound or disease, which needs healing and binding up, and which consists in a proneness and inclination to the like acts.

Now though the guilt of sin is taken away upon our repentance, yet the stain and the scar remain still, in part, and these need daily renewing. And because a new guilt may be contracted by new sins, therefore we have daily need of pardon and remission.

The necessity of this inward renewing appears in three ways—
1. Because of the corruption which naturally lodges in the heart, and so pollutes the whole man, here is that gall which imbitters all our actions—here is that leaven which sours the whole lump—here is that leprosy which defiles body and soul, so that from the head (the understanding) to the sole of the feet (the affections), all is full of sores (Isa. 1:6) If the tongue is a "world of wickedness," what is the heart like? If there is a "beam in the eye," what

must there be in the heart?

2. If it is not renewed, it is the most dangerous enemy we have. It is "deceitful above all things and desperately wicked," says the prophet (Jer.17:9). It can deceive us without the help of Satan. But he can do nothing without the heart, he must plow with our heifer—it is more near to us than to Satan, a part of ourselves. "Resist the Devil and he will flee from us," but if we resist to the utmost, yet this deceiver will stick close to us. Satan tempts and leaves us for a time, but this tempter never leaves us. This is like a treacherous person in the city, who opens the gates and lets in the enemy, who otherwise could not have entered by force.

3. It is the fountain of all our actions. None are accepted which do not come from a pure heart. If this is polluted, all our actions are abominable. Whatever an unclean person touched, under the Law, was unclean. So whatever actions we perform, though good in themselves, if the heart is not renewed and cleansed, they are polluted by it.

IF WE ARE TO BE RENEWED, WE MUST USE MEANS

1. We must wash our hearts with tears of repentance, as David did after his great fall, and as St. Peter did after he had denied his Master. This potion of repentance will purge our the infectious humors. It is true, "the blood of Christ cleanses from all sin" (1 John 1:7), it takes away the guilt, and the Spirit of God renews the heart, in respect to the stain (You are washed, you are sanctified in the name of the Lord Jesus and by the Spirit of our God). But neither Christ or His Spirit will come and dwell in an impure heart. If the heart is not prepared by repentance, we cannot apply the blood of Christ to take away the guilt. There are preparatory works wrought by the assistance of the Spirit, as sorrow and remorse for sin, before the Spirit comes to dwell in us. And Christ "stands at the door and knocks" by preparatory acts of grace before He will come in and sup with us.

2. We must avoid all occasions of sin. "If our right eye offend us, we must pluck it out; if our hand offend us, we must cut if off" (Matt. 5:29). We must part with anything, though it be never so dear to us, if it is an occasion to sin. We must shun and avoid all evil company. David says that "all his delight was in the saints, and in those who excelled in virtue." He "was a companion to all those who feared the name of God." As for the wicked, he would "not allow them to come into his sight," nay, he "would not make mention of them in his lips." (Ps. 16:3, 119, 101:7). We must also avoid idleness! David was idle when he was tempted to uncleanness. Idleness is the Devil's pillow. An idle person is a standing puddle, apt to stagnate and putrefy. This makes the soil fit for Satan to sow his seed in. Therefore it was good counsel which said, Let

Satan always find you alert and ready.

3. We must watch over our outward senses, for they are the windows by which sinful objects are conveyed into the heart, and by which sinful lusts are stirred up in the soul. Do not look on the tree lest you be taken with the pleasant look of the fruit. We must pray with the Psalmist that "God would turn away our eyes from beholding vanity," and as Job did, make a "covenant with our eyes" not to look upon ensnaring objects. We must "stop our ears against the charms" of the Devil. The ear is apt to receive evil speeches which it conveys to the heart, and therefore we "must take heed what we hear." (Ps. 119:37; Job 31:1; 1 Cor. 15:33, Ps. 58:5, Mark 4:25).

4. Suppress the first motions of sin as soon as they arise in the heart. This is to crush the cockatrice in the egg. This is easy at first, but it is difficult if we give way to them. Though they seem small, yet they are bad and make way for worse. Evil thoughts not resisted bring delight; delight breeds consent, consent brings action, action begets custom and custom necessity. Therefore we must dash them to pieces when they are young, before they grow too strong! We must not once "consult with flesh and blood," as the a break of water at the first (lest if they break out it may be too late), so we must stop sinful motions at the first, before they gather strength and so make us unable to resist them.

5. The word of God has a specific virtue to cleanse the heart. "Let the word of Christ dwell in you plentifully," or richly (Col. 3:16). "The word of the Lord is clean" and there the question "with what shall a young man cleanse his way?" is answered "by taking heed according to Thy word." (Psalm 119:9).

6. The heart must be weaned from the pleasures and delights of the world. There must be such a weaning that we may say with David, "I have behaved myself as one that is weaned from his mother's breast." (Ps. 131:2). This must be by meditating of the vanity and shortness, the insufficiency of all earthly pleasures. As Abner said to Joab, they bring bitterness at the last. These sweet waters end in the brackish salt sea. These short, momentary pleasures will be rewarded with endless torments. The rich man received in his lifetime "his good things," and Lazarus "evil," but now, says Abraham, "Lazarus is comforted, and your are tormented."

7. We must with the Apostle "keep the body under, bring it into subjection." He that besieges an enemy will cut off provision from him. Those fleshly lusts "which war against the soul" will not be vanquished if we pamper the body, for by this means they are very much strengthened (1 Peter 2:11). Therefore we must avoid all excess in food or drink, and whatever may be a provocation or

incitement to our lusts. "Fullness of bread and abundance of idleness" were the sins of Sodom. And Solomon gives counsel not "to tarry at the wine," his reason being, "your eyes will behold strange women." We must take heed then of pampering the body, if we do not desire to have those lusts grow in our hearts. And if we have in any way neglected our duty in this, we must with the Apostle "take revenge upon ourselves" (2 Cor. 7:11) for our excess, by some penal exercises, such as fasting, watching, prayer, etc. This is both to show our repentance for our going beyond what is right and reasonable, and to keep the body more in subjection for the future. And though this may seem to be a hard thing to flesh and blood, yet by the power of Christ and His Spirit we shall be able to perform it.

SO WE MUST KEEP OUR HEARTS WITH ALL DILIGENCE

As Solomon exhorts, we must keep our hearts with all diligence and labor for purity of heart (Proverbs 4:23). And if we do so, we shall be fitted for communion with God (who is a God of pure eyes which cannot look upon iniquity) by faith here, and by clear vision hereafter.

"Blessed are the pure in heart, for they shall see God." These are the very words of Christ.

FINIS

PUBLISHER'S NOTE: If you have read and benefited from reading these remarks by this grand old Puritan father, write us to encourage more excerpts of helpful treatises in future books.
Thank you.